Celtic CHAMPIONS

© Published in Great Britain in 2012 by Trinity Mirror Sport Media,
PO Box 48, Old Hall Street, Liverpool L69 3EB.
All rights reserved. This magazine has been sold
subject to the condition that it may not be reproduced, stored in a retrieval
system or transmitted in any form or by any means, electronic, mechanical,
photocopying, recording or otherwise without the publisher's prior consent.
ISBN: 9781908695253

Photographic credits: SNS Pix, PA Pics
Executive Editor: Ken Rogers
Senior Editor: Steve Hanrahan
Senior Art Editor: Rick Cooke
Senior Production Editor: Paul Dove
Magazine Editor: Paul Cuddihy
Deputy Magazine Editor: Joe Sullivan
Sub Editor: Michael McGuinness
Writers: Laura Brannan, Mark Henderson, Tony Hamilton
Design: Vicky Andrews, Lee Ashun,
Alison Barkley, Matthew Barnes, Zoë Bevan,
Graeme Helliwell, Michael McGuinness
Cover Design: Rick Cooke

Printed By: William Gibbons

Celtic Football Club,
Celtic Park, Glasgow G40 3RE
Celtic plc Directors Ian Bankier,
Peter Lawwell, Eric Riley, Dermot Desmond,
Tom Allison, Brian Duffy, Brian Wilson, Ian Livingston
CFAC Directors Peter Lawwell, Eric Riley,
John Keane, Michael McDonald, Kevin Sweeney
Manager Neil Lennon
Assistant Manager Johan Mjallby
Football Development Manager John Park
Head of Youth Chris McCart
**Club Doctor and Head of Sport and
Exercise Medicine** Dr Roddy Macdonald
Head Physiotherapist Tim Williamson
Head Fitness Coach Kenny McMillan
Kit Controller John Clark

Contact
Celtic Football Club 0871 226 1888
(Calls cost up to 10p per minute, telecoms provider
dependent. Mobile and other provider charges may vary)

NEIL LENNON – CELTIC LEGEND

**IT is an illustrious and exclusive group of men…
Willie Maley, Jimmy McGrory, Jock Stein, Billy
McNeill, Davie Hay, Wim Jansen, Martin O'Neill and
Gordon Strachan.**

To that list is now added Neil Lennon, having secured his first league title as Celtic manager.

Having already established himself as a legend in the green and white Hoops, the Irishman has now ensured his place alongside the managerial legends of Celtic Football Club. And as someone who knows the history of the club, it's an achievement he is very proud of.

"This means everything," he explained. "It was the best day in my professional life. For the last two years I've felt like I've been on probation.

"People made me unsure if I was justified in being the Celtic manager because I was so inexperienced, but they're going to have to take me more seriously now. There's a lot more substance than a lot of people think.

"We should enjoy this. It's our first title in four years. I've won a few championships as a player but this means more to me that any of the others because I'm the manager.

"It can be a lonely job at times. You have to find a lot of answers, but it's all worth it in the end. To walk alongside Mr Stein, Billy McNeill, Davie Hay, Wim Jansen, Martin and Gordon is a very special feeling."

Having won five league titles as a Celtic player, Neil Lennon knew what was required of his players to get over that finishing line. As a manager, the responsibilities are multiplied tenfold, while the pressure also intensifies. It's understandable, therefore, that the success tastes all the sweeter.

The Irishman came so close to winning the championship last season, when his side lost out by a solitary point. At the last home game of the 2010/11 campaign, the Celtic manager declared to an emotional Paradise that 'This is not the end, this is only the beginning…'

Eleven months on, his words have proved prophetic as his Celtic side wrapped up the league title with five games to spare, turning on the style to beat Kilmarnock 6-0 at Rugby Park.

"We built a young, vibrant squad from the remnants of 2010 and came very close last year which was a nice surprise because we were so far behind the year before," he added. "There was a real motivation to go one better this year, though and they've done it in spectacular fashion.

"The performance at Rugby Park epitomised the team - it was exciting, fast, young, energetic and full of quality. In the last couple of weeks we looked a bit mentally tired but the win over St Johnstone last week set the game at Kilmarnock up.

"Everyone came to party, but the players still had to go out to perform and they did that in emphatic fashion. I'm so pleased we did it in the style we did. It was breathtaking.

"I think the whole season was encapsulated in that one game at Rugby Park. They're vibrant, they're young, they're naive at times but you have to understand that with young players. But what an achievement."

Indeed, it has been a remarkable achievement by a squad with an average age of 23. There were times in the early part of the season when it looked as though the title challenge was coming off the rails, but a steady nerve and steely determination, which emanated from the manager and his backroom staff, produced a remarkable turnaround in fortunes.

Rugby Park was the scene of jubilant celebrations in April, but back in October last year, it had almost been the death knell for Celtic's championship aspirations.

Trailing 3-0 at half-time, all looked lost, but a galvanising half-time team-talk from the manager and a courageous second-half fight-back from the players saw them rescue an unlikely point. But it was from such small beacons of >

"IT'S been a long time coming. We knew we would win the league finally but it's great to finish it off in style. I thought we were tremendous and the players have been brilliant.

"They have turned it around and showed how they are mentally strong. Some people outside the club had questioned that but now they are there, it's well-deserved and hopefully we can keep them together for a long time.

"They showed their true talent on Saturday and how well they can play. Over the course of the season they have been tremendous. They were so mentally strong and have worked so hard for one another to come back from when we were 15 points behind.

"When we first came in, especially Neil, we knew we had to turn around things as we hadn't won the league for a number of years. And now we have won the championship and that has always been the main focus this season. You could see from the scenes how much it means to everybody.

"Sure, there have been questions now and then but throughout all the teams we have played the most games and have been defensively the best and attacking-wise, I think we are the best as well. So that shows we are the best side in Scotland.

"Obviously you can say the Kilmarnock game when we were 3-0 down and managed to come back for a draw was very important for us as right then we were under pressure with the gap in points. We weren't playing the best we could but after that we had a couple of games in Europe which we drew confidence from and then went on this fantastic run in this league.

"As a player, it's more of an explosive feeling when you win the league but when you work in management there is more thought and you are bit more laid-back about things when it happens as you still have games to think about.

"Hopefully the players right now are just bursting and are happy. We are obviously so happy as well but we still have an eye on the games coming up. It's a bit different but I'm so proud of the players and so happy to have achieved this in management as well at this great club. Every title is special in its own way."

- JOHAN MJALLBY

"Everyone came to the party, but the players still had to go out to perform and they did that in emphatic fashion. I'm so pleased we did it in the style we did. It was breathtaking"

— NEIL LENNON (April 2012)

> hope that the belief grew within the squad that they could go on and lift the title.

Weeks later, that hope still hung by a thread as the Hoops travelled to play Motherwell at Fir Park, trailing Rangers by 15 points. Anything other than a win would have been disastrous and, again, the Celtic players held their nerve, produced a 2-1 victory in a tight game and began a remarkable run of consecutive wins – 20 in all domestic competitions, including 17 in the SPL.

That form saw Celtic cut into Rangers' lead to the extent that, by the time the teams met at Celtic Park on December 28, victory for the home side put them on top of the table. It's a position they have not relinquished since.

"This is a really young team we have here but they're a joy to work with," said the Celtic manager. "I look back to what I was doing when I was the same age as the likes of Adam Matthews and James Forrest.

"I was at Crewe in front of maybe 3,000 or 4,000 people, under no pressure. These guys are doing it front of 60,000 every other week, with huge expectations.

"Not only have they got the talent but they have great temperaments as well. It's a young side and we're building something we think is special.

"They are talented players, and sometimes with them being young they tail off a little bit, and I understand that, but to achieve this success with a squad as young as this fills me with even more pride.

One thing that Neil Lennon is well aware of is the different reactions to success as a player and as a manager. While players can savour each triumph for longer, a manager's attention is already turning towards the next match, the next tournament, the next challenge.

And the Celtic manager is already looking to the future and the prospect of delivering Champions League football back to Paradise. Celtic will enter the UEFA Champions League third qualifying round in the summer and progressing to the group stages of the competition is a huge aim.

"We played well in Europe and the Udinese game was a shot in the arm at a time when we needed it," Neil Lennon said. "We've gone away and played ever so well and there were fantastic individual performances against a class side.

"We'll take that on board. We have the Champions League qualifiers in July. They're vital to our season so we need to sit down and really look at our close-season programme and then our pre-season and try to get it right. And it's important to Scottish football that we try and get into the group stage and make a fist of it after that."

But if Neil Lennon does allow himself some time to take stock of what he's achieved this season, then who could begrudge him such an indulgence. The pressures of managing Celtic have been compounded by everything that he's had to endure away from the game.

Bringing success to the club in those trying circumstances makes it an even greater personal triumph for him – and he was keen to thank those who has shown him support during times of difficulty.

"There are things outside the football that have affected my life and it's not always an easy thing to deal with," he said.

"It obviously takes a bit of strength to get through it but it takes a bit of support as well and I've got great support from my family, the players, the club, the board, Mr Desmond and Peter Lawwell, in particular.

"They've thrown everything at me but I'm now after 12 years with this club, at the pinnacle of my professional career, so I'm not going to go away in a hurry.

"It's been an emotional two years for me. To finish it off the way we did was brilliant."

Willie Maley: 1897/98

CELTIC had already won three league titles before they lifted their first one with Willie Maley in charge as secretary/manager. The man who played a pivotal role in the first 50 years of Celtic's existence had helped the club lift their first ever league title in 1892/93 as a player but now, in charge of the team, he steered them to a well-deserved title triumph, with the team remaining unbeaten throughout the course of the season.

The season began with a 4-1 home win over Hibernian, with debut Bhoy Adam Henderson scoring twice. And after a goal-less draw against Hearts in Edinburgh in the next game, the Celts quickly returned to winning ways with victories over St Bernard's, Clyde and then a 4-1 thumping of Rangers at Ibrox in September 1897. Indeed, Celtic drew three of their 18 league games – all of them 0-0 – while winning every other game. The last of those draws came in the final game of the season when Rangers were the visitors to Celtic Park.

Season 1897/98 also saw a Christmas Day game for the Celts, and it was a short trip along the road to Shawfield to play Clyde. The green and white stripes triumphed, beating the home side 9-1, with George 'Dod' Allan netting five festive crackers. Allan, who joined at the start of the season from Liverpool, ended as top goalscorer, scoring 15 league goals, and he returned to Merseyside at the end of the campaign. Tragically, he contracted tuberculosis soon after and died in October 1899 at the age of just 24.

While Celtic's league campaign remained unblemished by defeat, their Scottish Cup campaign lasted all of two games. Having beaten Arthurlie 7-0, atoning slightly for the ignominy of the previous season's defeat against the junior outfit, the Celts were then eliminated by Third Lanark.

However, that title was the start of a long litany of silverware brought to Celtic Park right up until 1940. This included the historic six-in-a-row triumph between 1904-10, which was quickly followed by four consecutive league titles between 1913-17. And Maley was also responsible for bringing 'some great names to the game', including Patsy Gallacher and a man who would later become Celtic manager, the legendary goalscorer, Jimmy McGrory, whose 468 goals in 445 games remain a record unlikely ever to be beaten.

WILLIE MALEY HONOURS

League Championships (16)
1897/98 1904/05, 1905/06, 1906/07, 1907/08, 1908/09, 1909/10, 1913/14, 1914/15, 1915/16, 1916/17, 1918/19, 1921/22, 1925/26, 1935/36, 1937/38

Scottish Cups (14)
1899, 1900, 1904, 1907, 1908, 1911, 1912, 1914, 1923, 1925, 1927, 1931, 1933, 1937

Empire Exhibition Trophy
1938

SCOTTISH LEAGUE DIVISION ONE 1897/98

	PLD	W	D	L	F	A	PTS
CELTIC	**18**	**15**	**3**	**0**	**56**	**13**	**33**
Rangers	18	13	3	2	71	15	29
Hibernian	18	10	2	6	47	29	22
Hearts	18	8	4	6	54	33	20
Third Lanark	18	8	2	8	37	38	18
St Mirren	18	8	2	8	30	36	18
Dundee	18	5	3	10	29	36	13
Partick Thistle	18	6	1	11	34	64	13
St Bernard's	18	4	1	13	35	67	9
Clyde	18	1	3	14	21	83	5

CAPTAIN'S HONOUR AT LEADING CELTS TO TITLE

SCOTT Brown has won the league title before with Celtic as part of Gordon Strachan's squad in the 2007/08 season. He enjoyed that success but this time around it's even sweeter, and not just because he's now club captain.

A costly suspension in the title run-in saw the midfielder miss a number of vital games and he only came on as a substitute in the title-clinching match at Tannadice.

Brown learned a lesson that season, and with a superb disciplinary record that saw him pick up just two yellow cards in this league campaign, he ensured he didn't miss out on the march to the title.

And as a key member of Neil Lennon's squad, Brown's presence in the heart of the team has been an important factor in securing the championship.

"It's a great honour to win the league and to win it as the Celtic captain is even better," Brown said. "The way we've turned things around this season shows the determination of the lads and how close we are as a group.

"It shows the great team spirit and the dressing room is a great place to be around – that's not because of the gaffer or one person

individually, we've all come together really well and enjoy each other's company.

"The scenes at Rugby Park showed some of the newer boys what kind of club this is to play for. And I don't think they expected anything like that crowd to be outside Celtic Park waiting for us, especially when we don't even have the trophy.

"Just to turn up to see us is incredible and they have really spurred us on. Right from the first week of the season the fans been incredible and it's an honour to play in front of them. They've been behind us the whole time."

And like his team-mates, the Celtic captain reserved much of his praise for one man – the manager, Neil Lennon.

"This title is more for the gaffer than anyone else," he said. "What he's been through this season and last, it's not very nice for anyone, but he's dealt with it really well and taken it on his chin. He's got stronger and stronger and went out in every game to prove everybody wrong.

"It's a great honour to be a winning Celtic captain, and if we play the way we did in the first-half at Rugby Park, there's not many teams in Britain who could stop us."

"IT'S amazing. This is the first time I have ever won a Championship. I have worked very hard this season to be a champion and it's worth it. It's a great honour for me.

"This is a big difference. Winning a cup is great but winning the league is huge and there was great motivation for every one. I think we deserved it this year so we just want to enjoy it.

"I'm still young and have things to learn but it's not easy to win the league anywhere in the world and this is my seventh year as a professional and now I have become a champion, so this has huge emotion for me.

"To play for Celtic is a big privilege for us. We wanted to give the fans a present as they always give us support. Even if we get a bad result they are always behind us, so we wanted to give something back to them.

"It was a great day. I think we played very well. Before the game, the gaffer had just told us to enjoy it and we just proved we are the champions and the best in the league.

"I have been here for three years and now I have become a champion. Sometimes there have been bad days and sometimes there have been good days but this year individually and as part of a team it's been a perfect season.

"I think the Kilmarnock game was the turning point in the season. We were losing 3-0 and got it back to 3-3. After that we just kept going and winning the games.

"We just wanted to give them a bit of revenge as well after the League Cup final. It was definitely the best game of this season. It was a great result."

- KI SUNG YUENG

"IT'S the best feeling. Everyone here feels happy in this moment and we've done this for ourselves, our families and the fans. I think we have done our jobs this season, every day in training and every game. I am so happy as, in the end, we have won the league.

"I missed a lot of games since I was injured at the start of the January but the players have done a good job in every game and in training. I wanted to come back and help but I think the players have done their job very well and have won the league which is so important.

"I think we don't just have good players and good talent we have good personnel here. Everyone in the club wants to be the best. We have a good team and a good group and together we want to win everything and every game. We have just continued to do that and hopefully we can do that in the semi-final and then hopefully the cup final as well. To win the double this season would be a big thing for me and everyone here.

"I always say that Celtic have a big support and amazing fans. They are our number 12 or number one. I think the fans are fantastic."

- BERAM KAYAL

JOE, JOE, SUPER JOE!

THERE might have been times when Joe Ledley has been referred to as 'an unsung hero', but the Celtic fans soon put an end to that term with regular bursts of 'Joe, Joe Super Joe!' ringing out around ground throughout Scotland.

Because the fans can see that the Welsh internationalist is a vital player in Neil Lennon's side and one who has been instrumental in driving Celtic to the title.

His work-rate is exceptional, his attitude first-class in playing whatever position is asked of him, and his contribution in terms of goals scored and created cannot be under-estimated. In short, he is Super Joe.

And having endured the disappointment of missing out on the title run-in last season through injury, which also saw the Hoops pipped at the post, Ledley is delighted to have

secured the championship this time around.

"It's a fantastic feeling and obviously well-deserved as well after the way we've played football this season," Ledley said. "We had a slow start but credit to the boys, we stuck together and worked hard week in, week out and we proved at Rugby Park how well we can play football.

"There was a lot of pressure on us, and we're only young, but we owed everyone this after losing the League Cup final. We went out there and played and dealt with the occasion very well. We knew when we got the first two we could go on and get more, the boys were fantastic.

"Charlie has been fantastic this season and he proved it again against Kilmarnock. It was great to see Loovey get a goal as well, he hasn't played much this season but he's been

magnificent week-in-week-out in training so deserves his chance. He was fantastic and it was nice to see us scoring from all over the pitch."

And Ledley also emphasised that this championship is a well-deserved one for Celtic who have, over the course of the season, proved themselves to be the SPL's top team.

The character and quality of Neil Lennon's squad has been evident for all but the blindest to see, and the way they overturned a 15-point deficit says much about the team spirit at Celtic.

"We were unlucky last year but this year we've proven we're the best," said Ledley. "We play the best football and we have the best players. We're the best team in Scotland. This is a great achievement for us and the fans."

"IT feels brilliant. It's the best feeling in football. Being my first season, I couldn't have dreamt for it to be any better. We have won the title with seven games left.

"It's obviously brilliant but the team have been fantastic all year and even though we have won the title now, we just want to keep this going for the rest of the season.

"We couldn't really have dreamt for it to go any better. We were 4-0 up at half-time and I thought first half was the best we have played the whole season.

"When you are playing an away game and you have three stands full of your fans, it's absolutely brilliant. They drove us on, especially the first half, and were great the whole game.

"Kilmarnock beat us in the League Cup as well so it was a nice bit of revenge as well. I think our average age is 24 so we have plenty more years left in us and I think if we keep this group of players together we will have a great chance of winning successive titles."

- ADAM MATTHEWS

"IT'S hard to put into words what this means to me. After losing it last season, on the last day, by a point, after thinking we deserved it, to come and do what we've done this season, in the style in which we've done it, even though people were writing us off in October/November, it feels absolutely fantastic.

"All credit to Neil Lennon and the players, a big group of them have been sensational. It's hard to pick individuals but as a squad and a group of guys they are a credit to the football club.

"We always thought we had the ability, the character and the strength and depth in the squad to go on and close the gap. On the whole we knew we could do it, we had the players capable of doing it - myself, Neil, Johan and Gary knew we could do it and we proved it.

"This is a victory for Neil as well, and he'll be immensely proud of when he sits down in a day or two and reflects on what has happened. I know his mum and dad are here, they've not been across all season and they'll be proud of him. We're proud of him as well. He's dragged us along, and the players along - he leads and we follow."

- ALAN THOMPSON

10 MATCHES WHICH DECIDED THE TITLE

KILMARNOCK 3-3 CELTIC
(Stokes 73, 76, Mulgrew 80)
October 15, 2011

Without doubt, the turning point in the entire campaign. Trailing 3-0 to the hosts after a calamitous opening 45 minutes, Celtic were not only in disarray, their season was in danger of complete collapse. Demoralised as they trooped off the pitch at the interval, there looked no way back for Celtic. However, showing magnificent spirit and resolve, the Hoops fought back and recorded a dramatic seven-minute turnaround. Anthony Stokes curled home a free-kick in the 73rd minute to provide a glimmer of hope. Three minutes later, that hope was transformed into serious belief as the Irishman rifled a shot into the corner from 25 yards. Celtic were galvanised, Kilmarnock were stunned. In the 80th minute, a free-kick was headed back across goal by Daniel Majstorovic and Charlie Mulgrew headed into the net, sending the Hoops support into raptures. Although the winner never arrived, the slide had been halted.

MOTHERWELL 1-2 CELTIC
(Stokes 14, Hooper 80)
November 11, 2011

Before the match, Celtic found themselves in third place behind the home side. Despite the spirited comeback at Kilmarnock, Celtic were 15 points adrift of Rangers. This was a must-win game. However, a rousing display in a 3-1 win over Rennes in the Europa League three days earlier had demonstrated a readiness to fight for the title. It was on display at Fir Park as well. Michael Higdon had put the hosts ahead with an early goal, but Stokes restored parity from close range soon after. It remained that way until the final 10 minutes. As the clock ticked down on the match along with Celtic's title aspirations, Paddy McCourt embarked on a mazy run and supplied Stokes. His cross from the left was turned home by Gary Hooper. As frustrations boiled over among the home ranks, Tim Clancy saw red for a petulant kick at Celtic's goalscorer.

CELTIC 5-0 ST MIRREN
(Samaras 4, Hooper 8, 53, 57, McGeouch 72)
November 26, 2011

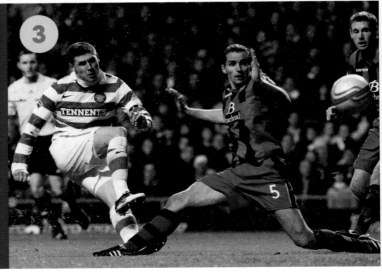

Buoyed by successive wins over Motherwell, Inverness CT and Dunfermline, Celtic's confidence was gradually returning. In just over two weeks, they had also whittled down Rangers' lead to seven points. And by the end of this match, there was no question that a revitalised Celtic were firmly back in the title hunt. Georgios Samaras broke the deadlock within five minutes when his low shot crept under Craig Samson, before the prolific Hooper bagged a hat-trick with three clinical finishes. Substitute Dylan McGeouch capped off a perfect day in Paradise by scoring a superb solo goal on his home debut, skipping past several players from deep inside his own half before drilling the ball beyond Samson. The following day Kilmarnock took the scalp of Rangers and the gap was now only a mere four points. The momentum was shifting.

CELTIC 1-0 HEARTS
(Wanyama 74)
December 10, 2011

The Hoops were seeking their sixth victory on the spin and fashioned all the early openings and dominating possession. However, an early goal was not forthcoming against a dogged visiting defence. After Stokes sent a header crashing off the underside of the bar from James Forrest's delivery, it looked like it would be an afternoon of frustration for the hosts. From an unlikely source, however, Celtic broke the deadlock. Charlie Mulgrew's free-kick had been blocked and there appeared little cause for concern for Hearts when it bounced beside Victor Wanyama. But the Kenyan midfielder casually drew back his right-foot and powered a shot into the top corner. It was a wonderful strike but he looked set to be denied the winning goal when the Tynecastle side were awarded a controversial penalty in added time. Fraser Forster was the hero, though, pushing Eggert Jonsson's penalty to safety with seconds remaining.

4

5

CELTIC 2-1 KILMARNOCK
(Samaras 45, 53)
Saturday, December 24, 2011

Celtic welcomed Kilmarnock to Paradise, knowing a victory could put them within a point of Rangers ahead of the derby clash four days later. The Ibrox side had been consigned to defeat in the early kick-off by St Mirren in Paisley, and having being handed that early Christmas present, there was huge incentive for the Hoops to collect the full spoils. On the stroke of half-time, Georgios Samaras broke Kilmarnock's resistance, heading home from Cha Du Ri's cross. The Greek striker doubled his tally after the break, firing beyond Cammy Bell after being supplied by Hooper. The points seemed secure but a ferocious finish from Danny Raachi in the closing minutes caused a few nervous moments before the final whistle sounded to signal Celtic's eighth league win in a row, setting them perfectly for the visit of Rangers.

CELTIC 1-0 RANGERS
(Ledley 54)
December 28, 2011

Celtic had been written off as title contenders less than two months earlier, having fallen 15 points behind their rivals in the race for the Championship. Yet here they were, with a chance of ending 2011 on the SPL summit. They were determined to seize their chance. Driving winds made conditions treacherous on a bitter winter's night and Celtic had Fraser Forster to thank in the first-half for a terrific save from Lee Wallace's header. However, Celtic upped the tempo after the break and dominated thereafter. And they were rewarded in the 52nd minute as Joe Ledley put the Hoops ahead after a sustained spell of pressure. The Welshman rose highest to connect powerfully with Charlie Mulgrew's deep corner. Paradise erupted. Rangers had ample time to level proceedings but found the Celtic backline in resolute form. In the end, it was a comfortable victory and the perfect way to end 2011.

6

7

ST MIRREN 0-2 CELTIC
(Forrest 71, Brown 88)
January 21, 2012

Having reached the top of the SPL, Celtic were determined to stay there but early in 2012, they faced a trip to Paisley which appeared to satisfy the conditions of a possible slip-up - dreadful weather and a confident home side. Both sides had chances in the opening half, including a spectacular strike by Hooper from 35 yards which forced Craig Samson into a super stop. Forster had made two fine saves after the break before the introduction of Kris Commons and Anthony Stokes gave the Hoops fresh impetus. And in the 70th minute, Forrest fired Celtic ahead from the edge of the box. With minutes remaining, Brown settled matters with a wonderful, curling left-foot shot, reminiscent of his goal against Rangers in 2010/11. Another tough test had been negotiated. Later in the day, the Ibrox side lost further ground by drawing 1-1 with Aberdeen. Celtic's lead was now four points.

HEARTS 0-4 CELTIC
(Brown 3, Wanyama 20, Ledley 31, Hooper 60)
February 8, 2012

Neil Lennon described this display as probably the best in his time as manager and there was sound evidence for this assertion. Back in October, Celtic had suffered a disappointing 2-0 defeat at the same ground in their most difficult period of the season. On this occasion, they were simply sensational, playing with an intensity, fluency and pace which their opponents couldn't live with. Just 30 seconds after surviving a scare, when Stephen Elliot's header appeared to have crossed the line, Brown rifled Celtic into the lead at the other end. Wanyama soon doubled the advantage with an accurate finish, before Ledley capped off another sweeping move on the half-hour mark. In the second-half, Celtic continued to threaten and Hooper finally added number four as he turned in Wanyama's knockdown in front of a jubilant Celtic support. It was win number 13 on the spin for Celtic and arguably the most impressive of the lot.

HIBERNIAN 0-5 CELTIC
(Stokes 14, Hooper 20, 52, Mulgrew 47, Ki 77)
February 19, 2012

Coming 11 days after the resounding win over Hearts, this proved be another profitable trip to the capital for Celtic. With Rangers entering administration and losing to Kilmarnock the previous day, Neil Lennon's men had the carrot of going 17 points in front of their city rivals if they could win at Easter Road. And once Stokes, the scourge of his former employers yet again, had headed them in front in the 14th minute, the result was never in doubt. The striker turned provider six minutes later as Hooper made it 2-0, following a flowing counter-attack. In the second-half, Celtic maintained their momentum and sealed the points. A trademark Mulgrew free-kick made it 3-0 before Hooper added his second in the 52nd minute. A fortuitous finish from Ki, directing Commons' shot past Graham Stack, compounded the home side's misery as a euphoric Hoops support started to see the title coming into vision.

KILMARNOCK 0-6 CELTIC
(Mulgrew 8, 35, Loovens 17, Hooper 45, 89, Ledley 88)
April 7, 2012

Celtic secured the league title in emphatic style, beating Kilmarnock 6-0 at Rugby Park in front of over 14,000 jubilant Celtic supporters who had turned the stadium into a sea of green and white. Charlie Mulgrew got the party going with a goal after just eight minutes, heading home from a corner, and he turned provider just nine minutes later, crossing for Glenn Loovens to make it 2-0. Mulgrew then scored the pick of the bunch on 35 minutes, cutting inside from the left and firing a right-foot shot into the far corner. And on the stroke of half-time, he supplied another cross, this time for Gary Hooper to score. In the second-half, it was just a matter of counting down the clock to the final whistle, but in the last few minutes Joe Ledley and Gary Hooper added further goals to make it 6-0 for the Champions.

Jimmy McGrory: 1953/54

JIMMY McGrory's tenure as Celtic manager did not bring the same level of success that he enjoyed as a player. True, it was hard to produce any achievement that would match 468 goals in 445 games for the Hoops, but his time in charge at the club from the end of the Second World War until Jock Stein's arrival in 1965, was not a particularly successful one for Celtic. McGrory also had to contend with an unprecedented and completely unhelpful level of boardroom interference, which stopped immediately when Stein took over.

There were some high points, however, and the 7-1 victory over Rangers in the 1957 League Cup final remains one of the club's greatest ever results. McGrory's Celtic side also lifted the league title in season 1953/54, and just for good measure they also won the Scottish Cup that season for an impressive double.

The portents for the season were good, with Celtic winning the Coronation Cup in 1953 against all the odds, given they had finished eighth in the league the previous season. And one of the heroes of that unique trophy triumph, Neilly Mochan, who had joined the club just before the tournament started, provided the goals which won the title for Celtic, hitting 20 league goals. This tally included the only goal of the game on New Year's Day as the Hoops beat Rangers.

The nearest title challengers that season were actually Hearts, who finished five points behind Celtic in second place, while Partick Thistle were third. The Hoops also enjoyed a 7-1 win that season, beating Clyde by that scoreline at Shawfield on Boxing Day, while in a 3-0 win over Aberdeen in September, Bobby Collins scored a hat-trick of penalties.

"The portents for the season were good, with Celtic winning the Coronation Cup in 1953 against all the odds given they had finished eighth in the league the previous season"

The title secured, Celtic also lifted the Scottish Cup, beating Aberdeen 2-1 in the final at Hampden. Jimmy McGrory, the gentleman of Celtic Football Club, now had a title as manager to go with the three he won as a player. But the title would not return to Celtic Park until 12 years later in what would be the start of a golden era for the club.

JIMMY McGRORY HONOURS

League Championships (1)
1953/54

Scottish Cups (2)
1951, 1954

League Cup (2)
1956/57, 1957/58

Coronation Cup
1953

SCOTTISH LEAGUE DIVISION ONE 1953/54

	PLD	W	D	L	F	A	PTS
CELTIC	30	20	3	7	72	29	43
Hearts	30	16	6	8	70	45	38
Partick Thistle	30	17	1	12	76	54	35
Rangers	30	13	8	9	56	35	34
Hibernian	30	15	4	11	72	51	34
East Fife	30	13	8	9	55	45	34
Dundee	30	14	6	10	46	47	34
Clyde	30	15	4	11	64	67	34
Aberdeen	30	15	3	12	66	51	33
Q of the South	30	14	4	12	72	58	32
St Mirren	30	12	4	14	44	54	28
Raith Rovers	30	10	6	14	56	60	26
Falkirk	30	9	7	14	47	61	25
Stirling Albion	30	10	4	16	39	62	24
Airdrie	30	5	5	20	41	92	15
Hamilton	30	4	3	23	29	94	11

DOWNING THE DONS

October 23, 2011
Celtic 2-1 Aberdeen
(Ki, Mulgrew)

Charlie Mulgrew netted the winner against his former club as Celtic beat Aberdeen 2-1 at home. Ki Sung Yueng had given the Hoops a 17th-minute lead when he finished off a well-worked move, latching on to Gary Hooper's pass and firing low into the net. It was another game Celtic dominated in terms of possession, but the visitors equalised just before the hour-mark through Ryan Jack, though he would later receive his marching orders for a second booking. By that time, Celtic had restored their lead, and this time Ki was the provider. He fired in a free-kick on 72 minutes and Mulgrew was on hand to force the ball home to give Neil Lennon's side a 2-1 victory.

Man of the Match: Charlie Mulgrew

August 7, 2011
Aberdeen 0-1 Celtic
(Stokes)

The second game of the season saw Celtic on their travels again, this time to Pittodrie, and it proved to be a tough match for Neil Lennon's side. The Hoops suffered an early blow after just 17 minutes when Emilio Izaguirre, last season's Player of the Year, was stretchered off with a suspected broken ankle. His subsequent absence over the next few months was keenly felt. The only goal of the game came on 74 minutes from Anthony Stokes, who coolly slotted home from Kris Commons' pass. It was no more than the Hoops deserved against Aberdeen, having enjoyed the bulk of possession, after creating a plethora of chances.

Man of the Match:
Kris Commons

March 3, 2012
Aberdeen 1-1 Celtic
(Stokes)

Celtic's incredible run of consecutive SPL wins came to a halt when they were held to a 1-1 draw at Pittodrie. The Hoops had recorded 17 victories in a row to establish a commanding lead at the top of the table, and when Anthony Stokes fired home on 28 minutes, latching on to a precise Kris Commons pass, it looked as though the Celts were heading for win No.18. But Aberdeen drew level thanks to a large slice of luck just before half-time. Gavin Rae's shot was going wide of the target but it took a cruel deflection off debut Bhoy Andre Blackman and ended up in the back of the net.

Man of the Match:
Charlie Mulgrew

CELTS IN STATS

AUGUST 7, 2011
ABERDEEN 0-1 CELTIC
(STOKES 74)

ABERDEEN (4-4-2) Gonzalez; McArdle, Considine, Arnason, Foster; Pawlett (Paton 72), Milsom, Osbourne, Magennis (Megginson 82); Mackie (Low 87), Vernon. Not Used: J. Brown, Robertson, Shaughnessy, J. Brown

CELTIC (4-4-2) Zaluska; Matthews, Majstorovic, K. Wilson, Izaguirre (Mulgrew 16); Commons, Kayal, Ki, Ledley (Forrest 63); Hooper, Stokes (Samaras 82). Not Used: Cervi, Samaras, Maloney, Wanyama, McCourt

MATCH STATS

Aberdeen		Celtic
38	Possession	62
3	Shots on Target	13
3	Shots off Target	12
11	Fouls (conceded)	9
5	Corners	5
2	Yellow cards	1
0	Red cards	0

OCTOBER 23, 2011
CELTIC 2-1 ABERDEEN
(KI, MULGREW)

CELTIC (4-3-1-2): Forster; Matthews, Loovens (Majstorovic 18) Mulgrew, Ledley; Kayal, Wanyama (McCourt 72), Ki; Forrest; Hooper, Stokes. Not Used: Zaluska, M Wilson, El Kaddouri, Cha, McGeouch

ABERDEEN (4-4-2) Gonzalez; Jack, Mawene, Considine, Foster; Arnasson, Osborne, Milsom, Fyvie; Vernon (Chalali 75), Fallon (Mackie 75) Not Used: Brown, McArdle, Clark, Magennis, Megginson

MATCH STATS

Celtic		Aberdeen
65	Possession	35
7	Shots on Target	1
8	Shots off Target	1
4	Fouls (conceded)	17
7	Corners	4
0	Yellow cards	5
0	Red cards	1

MARCH 3, 2012
ABERDEEN 1-1 CELTIC
(STOKES)

CELTIC (4-4-2) Forster; Lustig (Cha 68) Rogne, Wilson, Blackman (Wanyama 59); Forrest, Mulgrew, Ledley, Commons (McGeouch 66); Hooper, Stokes. Not used: Zaluska, McCourt, Loovens, Brozek

ABERDEEN (4-4-2) Brown; Jack, Reynolds, Considine, McArdle; Vernon, Arnason, Fyvie (Pawlett 70) Rae, Megginson; Fallon (Mawene 78). Not used: Langfield, Mackie, Chalali, Magennis, Uchechi

MATCH STATS

Aberdeen		Celtic
46	Possession	54
3	Shots on Target	5
5	Shots off Target	2
16	Fouls (conceded)	8
3	Corners	6
1	Yellow cards	2
0	Red cards	0

V

Tangerine dream

August 13, 2011
Celtic 5-1 Dundee United
(Stokes, Hooper, Ki, Ledley, Forrest)

Celtic's first home league game of the season saw the Hoops comprehensively beat Dundee United 5-1, with five different players getting on the scoresheet. Not surprisingly, Neil Lennon's side dominated proceedings in terms of possession, and they took the lead after four minutes when Anthony Stokes netted. Johnny Russell equalised just after the half-hour mark, but it took the Hoops two minutes to restore their lead, thanks to a Gary Hooper goal. After the break, it was one-way traffic and the home side added three more goals courtesy of Ki Sung Yeung with the pick of the five goals, Joe Ledley and an injury-time strike from James Forrest.

Man of the Match: Scott Brown

CELTS IN STATS

AUGUST 13, 2011
CELTIC 5-1 DUNDEE UNITED
(STOKES, HOOPER, KI,
LEDLEY, FORREST)

CELTIC (4-4-2): Zaluska; M. Wilson, Majstorovic, K. Wilson, Mulgrew; Brown, Ki, Ledley, Commons (Forrest 63); Stokes (McCourt 77), Hooper (Maloney 66). Not used: Cervi, Matthews, Wanyama, Samaras.

DUNDEE UNITED (4-4-2): Pernis; Dillon, Kenneth, Watson, Dixon; Flood (Gunning 77), Allan (Armstrong 68), Robertson, Rankin; Daly, Russell. Not used: Banks, Swanson, Douglas, Mackay-Steven, Dow.

MATCH STATS

Celtic		Dundee United
65	Possession	35
9	Shots on Target	3
8	Shots off Target	3
10	Fouls (conceded)	14
5	Corners	7
1	Yellow cards	3
0	Red cards	0

January 14, 2012
Celtic 2-1 Dundee United
(Hooper, Wanyama)

Celtic began this match in impressive style, scoring two goals inside the first 17 minutes. Gary Hooper made it three goals in three games against Dundee United with a strike on 12 minutes. The Englishman latched on to an Anthony Stokes' pass and raced into the penalty area before firing the ball beyond the United goalkeeper. Five minutes later, Victor Wanyama headed home an Emilio Izaguirre cross to make it 2-0, and at this stage, Neil Lennon's side were in command. John Rankin reduced the deficit five minutes after the break when he fired home a shot from 35 yards. And just eight minutes later, Fraser Forster had a good save to deny Jon Daly an equaliser.

Man of the Match:
Gary Hooper

DECEMBER 4, 2011
DUNDEE UNITED 0-1 CELTIC
(HOOPER)

CELTIC (4-4-2) Forster; Cha, Majstorovic, Loovens (Brown 67) Matthews; Forrest, Kayal, Wanyama, Samaras; Hooper, Stokes (Ki 78). Not Used : Zaluska, Bangura, McCourt, McGeouch, F Twardzik.

DUNDEE UNITED (4-5-1) Pernis; Neilson, Kenneth, Gunning, Dixon; Russell, Flood (83) Robertson (Armstrong 61), Rankin, Mackay-Steven (Dalla Valle 61); Daly. Not Used: Banks, Dillon, Watson, Douglas.

MATCH STATS

Dundee United		Celtic
65	Possession	35
7	Shots on Target	1
8	Shots off Target	1
4	Fouls (conceded)	17
7	Corners	4
0	Yellow cards	5
0	Red cards	1

JANUARY 14, 2012
CELTIC 2-1 DUNDEE UNITED
(HOOPER, WANYAMA)

CELTIC (4-4-2): Forster; Matthews, Rogne, Mulgrew, Izaguirre (Commons 77); Brown, Wanyama, Ledley, Samaras; Hooper, Stokes (Ki 65). Not used: Zaluska, Cha, K Wilson, McCourt, Keatings.

DUNDEE UNITED (4-4-2): Pernis; Neilson, Dillon, Kenneth, Dixon (Douglas 64); Flood, Mackay-Stevens (Swanson 77), Robertson, Rankin; Daly, Russell. Not used: Banks, Ryan, Armstrong, Dalla Valle, Dow.

December 4, 2011
Dundee United 0-1 Celtic
(Hooper)

A goal after 12 minutes was enough to give Celtic all three points in a closely-contested match. Gary Hooper was the goal hero for the Hoops, latching on to a James Forrest pass and firing beyond Dusan Pernis and into the net. Neil Lennon's side created a number of chances throughout the game but were unable to add to the lead. However, they remained resolute at the back, denying Dundee United too many opportunities, and were worthy of the victory. That win meant Celtic were just four points behind then leaders, Rangers, though that would soon change dramatically.

Man of the Match:
Victor Wanyama

MATCH STATS

Celtic		Dundee United
57	Possession	43
8	Shots on Target	3
3	Shots off Target	2
3	Fouls (conceded)	14
7	Corners	8
0	Yellow cards	2
0	Red cards	0

PAR
FOR THE
COURSE

November 23, 2011
Celtic 2-1 Dunfermline Athletic
(Hooper, Forrest)

The scoreline in this match doesn't give a true indication of the level of dominance Celtic enjoyed, but while the Hoops managed to score two early goals, they couldn't add to the total and Dunfermline managed to score one goal late in the match to reduce the deficit. Gary Hooper opened the scoring after just six minutes, latching on to a slack pass from Paul Willis, accelerating past a defender and then despatching the ball into the back of the net. And on 13 minutes, James Forrest doubled Celtic's lead. Hooper was the provider this time, back-heeling the ball into the path of Forrest to finish. Celtic even missed a penalty from Ki after the break before Andy Barrowman scored for the visitors with three minutes remaining.

Man of the Match: James Forrest

February 22, 2012
Celtic 2-0 Dunfermline Athletic
(Mulgrew, Forrest)

Dunfermline arrived at Celtic Park and parked the proverbial bus in front of their goal, but while they managed to limit the home side to just two goals, they offered very little by way of an attacking threat themselves. Charlie Mulgrew opened the scoring on 33 minutes, taking the ball from just inside the opposition half and then striding forward before firing the ball into the net from 35 yards. Celtic didn't manage to double their lead until the 75th minute, and it was substitute James Forrest who scored, sliding in at the far post to steer Gary Hooper's low cross into the Dunfermline net.

Man of the Match:
Ki Sung Yueng

January 2, 2012
Dunfermline Athletic 0-3 Celtic
(Stokes, Wanyama, Mulgrew)

Celtic began 2012 as league leaders, having beaten Rangers 1-0 in the last league match of 2011 to leapfrog their city rivals. And Neil Lennon's side produced a powerful display at East End Park, winning comfortably 3-0. Celtic's opening goal on 18 minutes was a superb effort from Stokes. A Charlie Mulgrew cross into the box was headed back towards the Irishman by Georgios Samaras, and from 20 yards out, he controlled it with his right foot, lifted it over the outstretched Smith and slotted it into the top corner of the net. Victor Wanyama made it 2-0 on 40 minutes, arriving at the far post to fire home Mulgrew's free-kick from close-range. And Mulgrew completed the scoring on 70 minutes with a trademark free-kick into the back of the net.

Man of the Match:
Victor Wanyama

CELTS IN STATS

NOVEMBER 23, 2011
CELTIC 2-1 DUNFERMLINE ATHLETIC
(HOOPER, FORREST)

CELTIC (4-4-2): Forster; Matthews, Wanyama, Majstorovic, Ledley; Forrest, Kayal, Ki, Commons (McCourt 45); Hooper, Stokes (Samaras 79). Not Used: Zaluska, El Kaddouri, Blackman, Fraser, McGeouch.

DUNFERMLINE (4-4-2): Gallagher; Dowie, Potter, Keddie, Burns; Willis (Cardle 60) Mason, Thomson (Boyle 60) Graham, Barrowman, Kirk (Buchanan 65). Not Used: Smith McDougall, Byrne, Young

MATCH STATS

Celtic		Dunfermline
75	Possession	25
7	Shots on Target	2
9	Shots off Target	4
10	Fouls (conceded)	11
2	Corners	4
1	Yellow cards	0
0	Red cards	0

JANUARY 2, 2012
DUNFERMLINE ATHLETIC 0-3 CELTIC
(STOKES, WANYAMA, MULGREW)

DUNFERMLINE (4-4-2): Smith, Boyle, Keddie, Potter, Dowie, Mason (Cardle 52), Hardie, Burns, Willis (Kirk 63), Graham, Barrowman. Not used: Goodfellow, Buchanan, Easton, Thomson, Young.

CELTIC (4-4-2): Forster: Matthews, Rogne, Mulgrew, Ledley; Forrest, Brown, Wanyama (Izaguirre 79), Samaras; Stokes, Hooper (Ki 66). Subs not used: Zaluska, K. Wilson, Cha, McCourt, Bangura.

MATCH STATS

Dunfermline		Celtic
41	Possession	59
0	Shots on Target	3
3	Shots off Target	5
10	Fouls (conceded)	4
1	Corners	6
2	Yellow cards	1
0	Red cards	0

FEBRUARY 22, 2012
CELTIC 2-0 DUNFERMLINE ATHLETIC
(MULGREW, FORREST)

CELTIC (4-4-2): Forster; Cha, K Wilson, Mulgrew, Izaguirre (Forrest 67); Brown (Brozek 78), Ledley, Ki, Commons; Hooper, Stokes (Samaras 67). Not used: Zaluska, Matthews, Majstorovic, McGeouch.

DUNFERMLINE (4-4-2): Smith; Dowie, Rutkiewicz, Keddie, Boyle; Graham, Thomson, Hutton, Burns, Cardle (Willis 61); Buchanan (Hardie 67). Not used: Goodfellow, McCann, Mason, McDougall, Byrne.

MATCH STATS

Celtic		Dunfermline
72	Possession	28
16	Shots on Target	3
11	Shots off Target	0
5	Fouls (conceded)	7
16	Corners	3
0	Yellow cards	1
0	Red cards	0

V

KINGS of the castle

February 8, 2012
Hearts 0-4 Celtic
(Brown, Wanyama, Ledley, Hooper)

Neil Lennon's side produced one of the most impressive performances of the season to comprehensively defeat Hearts 4-0 at Tynecastle. In a dramatic start to the game, Hearts thought they'd opened the scoring from an early corner, and though Joe Ledley and Fraser Forster cleared the ball off the line, TV replays showed it was over. From there Celtic went on the break to open the scoring through inspirational captain Scott Brown. Victor Wanyama doubled Celtic's lead on 20 minutes before Ledley got in on the midfield scoring act with a header just after the half-hour mark. Celtic's fourth of the night came on 60 minutes, when Gary Hooper fired home from close-range.

Man of the Match:
Victor Wanyama

December 10, 2011
Celtic 1-0 Hearts
(Wanyama)

Victor Wanyama opened his scoring account for Celtic in spectacular style, netting the only goal of the game on 72 minutes to give the Hoops a 1-0 home win over Hearts. The ball had dropped to the Kenyan midfielder and from 25 yards out, he fired home an unstoppable shot beyond Hearts goalkeeper, Marion Kello. But Celtic also had to rely on their own goalkeeper to ensure all three points remained at Paradise after the visitors were awarded a penalty in the last few minutes of the game after Wanyama was penalised for an apparent handball in the box. Eggert Jonsson stepped up but Fraser Forster produced a magnificent save to deny Hearts a point they barely deserved.

Man of the Match:
Charlie Mulgrew

October 2, 2011
Hearts 2-0 Celtic

A disappointing day at Tynecastle saw Celtic lose 2-0 and have Kris Commons red-carded towards the end of the game. Hearts took the lead just before the hour mark when Rudi Skacel latched on to a long cross from the right wing and struck the ball under Adam Matthews and Fraser Forster, hitting the far corner of the net. Celtic's immediate response was to bring on Anthony Stokes, but the Hoops were given a mountain to climb seven minutes later when Commons was shown a straight red card for a foul on Adrian Mrowiec. And it was the home side who doubled their lead on 82 minutes when Ryan Stevenson took advantage of some hesitant defending to score.

Man of the Match:
James Forrest

CELTS IN STATS

OCTOBER 2, 2011
HEARTS 2-0 CELTIC

HEARTS (4-2-3-1): MacDonald; Hamill, Zaliukas, Webster, Grainger; Black (Smith 87), Mrowiec; Skacel (Obua 77), Jonsson, Templeton (Novikovas 83); Stevenson. Not used: Balogh, Robinson, Elliot, McGowan.

CELTIC (4-4-2): Forster; Matthews (M Wilson 73), Majstorovic, Mulgrew, El Kaddouri (McCourt 78); Forrest, Ki, Wanyama, Commons; Bangura (Stokes 59), Hooper. Not used: Zaluska, Samaras, Rogne, Slane.

MATCH STATS

Hearts		Celtic
46	Possession	54
4	Shots on Target	7
3	Shots off Target	6
16	Fouls (conceded)	17
3	Corners	12
2	Yellow cards	1
0	Red cards	1

DECEMBER 10, 2011
CELTIC 1-0 HEARTS
(WANYAMA)

CELTIC (4-4-2): Forster; Cha, Loovens (Brown 46), Majstorovic, Mulgrew; Forrest, Kayal, Wanyama, Samaras; Hooper, Stokes (Bangura 90+2). Not used: Zaluska, K Wilson, Ki, McGeouch, F Twardzik.

HEARTS (4-2-3-1): Kello; Hamill, Zaliukas, McGowan, Robinson (Elliot 78); Black (Obua 78), Mrowiec; Taouil, Jonsson, Templeton (Driver 78); Stevenson. Not used: McDonald, Nouikovas, Skacel, Mullen.

MATCH STATS

Celtic		Hearts
55	Possession	45
5	Shots on Target	1
3	Shots off Target	3
9	Fouls (conceded)	14
7	Corners	6
0	Yellow cards	3
0	Red cards	0

FEBRUARY 8, 2012
HEARTS 0-4 CELTIC
(BROWN, LEDLEY, WANYAMA, HOOPER)

HEARTS (4-4-2): MacDonald, Hamill, McGowan, Webster, Zaliukas, Taouil, Robinson (Santana 71), Mrowiec, Grainger (Skacel 63); Driver (Glen 46), Elliot. Not used: Ridgers, Barr, Obua, Holt.

CELTIC (4-4-2): Forster; Matthews, Rogne (Majstorovic 63), K Wilson, Mulgrew; Forrest, Brown (Brozek 73), Wanyama, Ledley; Hooper (Stokes 66), Samaras. Not used: Zaluska, Cha, Ki, Commons.

MATCH STATS

Hearts		Celtic
46	Possession	54
3	Shots on Target	4
4	Shots off Target	8
9	Fouls (conceded)	12
6	Corners	10
4	Yellow cards	2
0	Red cards	0

Capital Gains

February 19, 2012
Hibernian 0-5 Celtic
(Stokes, Hooper 2, Mulgrew, Ki)

Anthony Stokes continued his record of having scored at Easter Road on every visit there as a Celtic player with a goal after just 14 minutes. It heralded a goalscoring spree for the Hoops, who fired in five past their shell-shocked hosts. Gary Hooper made it 2-0 on 20 minutes, and after the break he added his second of the game following a trademark Charlie Mulgrew free-kick just two minutes after the restart. And Ki Sung Yueng completed the scoring rather fortuitously, knocking home a mis-hit Kris Commons shot. But the scoreline didn't flatter a rampant Celtic side intent on pressing home their advantage at the top of the SPL table.

Man of the Match: Joe Ledley

July 24, 2011
Hibernian 0-2 Celtic
(Stokes, Ki Sung-Yueng)

Celtic's opening game of the season came in July as the new campaign began very early in the summer. But it was an impressive start for Neil Lennon's side as they beat Hibernian 2-0 at Easter Road in what was a comfortable victory. Anthony Stokes had the honour of scoring Celtic's first goal of the 2011/12 season after just 13 minutes of the match. A free-kick from Kris Commons dropped to the Irishman at the far post, and from a tight angle, he lifted into the top corner of the Hibs net. While the Hoops dominated proceedings, it took until 63 minutes to double their tally. Ki Sung Yueng latched on to a Stokes pass and drove the ball home from 20 yards out.

Man of the Match:
Ki Sung Yueng

October 29, 2011
Celtic 0-0 Hibernian

Having beaten Hibernian 4-1 at Easter Road the previous Wednesday in the League Cup, Celtic went into the weekend SPL home clash against the Edinburgh side full of confidence. But it proved to be a frustrating afternoon for Neil Lennon's side as they couldn't break down a resolute Hibs defence determined to put up a better showing that they had in the cup. Indeed, the visitors managed to create a few chances of their own, and Fraser Forster had to be alert on a number of occasions. The goal-less draw concluded a disappointing October for the Hoops who, by the time of their next league game on November 6, would be 15 points behind Rangers.

Man of the Match:
Mark Wilson

CELTS IN STATS

JULY 24, 2011
HIBERNIAN 0-2 CELTIC
(STOKES, KI SUNG-YUENG)

HIBERNIAN (4-4-2): Stack; Booth, Hanlon, O'Hanlon (Stephens 61), Murray (Crawford 84); Sproule, Thornhill, Stevenson (Galbraith 70), Wotherspoon; Palsson, O'Connor. Not used: Brown, Scott, Taggart, De Graaf.

CELTIC (4-4-2): Zaluska; M. Wilson, Loovens, K. Wilson, Izaguirre; Commons (Forrest 59), Ki, Kayal, Ledley; Hooper (Maloney 85), Stokes (Samaras 78). Not used: Cervi, Mulgrew, Matthews, Wanyama.

MATCH STATS

Hibernian		Celtic
41	Possession	59
0	Shots on Target	6
0	Shots off Target	4
15	Fouls (conceded)	15
0	Corners	6
1	Yellow cards	0
0	Red cards	0

OCTOBER 29, 2011
CELTIC 0-0 HIBERNIAN

CELTIC (4-4-2): Forster; M Wilson, Rogne, Mulgrew, Matthews; Forrest, Kayal (Wanyama 33), Ledley, Ki (McCourt 70); Stokes, Hooper (Samaras 84). Not used: Zaluska, Cha, El Kaddouri, Majstorovic.

HIBS (4-2-2): Stack; Hanlon, O'Hanlon, Stephens, Wotherspoon; Galbraith, Stevenson, Osbourne, Agogo (Sproule 78); O'Conner (Thornhill 78), Griffiths (Palsson 89). Not used: Brown, Welsh, Sodje, Scott.

MATCH STATS

Celtic		Hibernian
65	Possession	35
7	Shots on Target	1
8	Shots off Target	1
4	Fouls (conceded)	17
7	Corners	4
0	Yellow cards	5
0	Red cards	1

FEBRUARY 19, 2012
HIBERNIAN 0-5 CELTIC
(STOKES, HOOPER 2, MULGREW, KI)

HIBERNIAN (4-4-2): Stack; Doherty (Francomb 46), McPake, Hanlon, Kujabi; Wotherspoon, Osbourne, Claros, Stevenson; Griffiths (O'Donovan 73), Doyle (O' Connor 51). Not Used: Brown, O'Hanlon, Scott, Sproule.

CELTIC (4-4-2): Forster; Matthews, Rogne (Izaguirre 71), K Wilson, Mulgrew; Forrest, Brown, Wanyama (Ki 55) Ledley; Hooper (Commons 61), Stokes. Not Used: Zaluska, Samaras, Majstorovic, Brozek.

MATCH STATS

Hibernian		Celtic
39	Possession	61
1	Shots on Target	9
8	Shots off Target	3
10	Fouls (conceded)	12
4	Corners	5
2	Yellow cards	1
0	Red cards	0

HIGHLAND FLINGS

February 11, 2012
Celtic 1-0 Inverness CT
(Ledley)

Celtic maintained their impressive run of league victories with a 1-0 win over Inverness CT at home, courtesy of a Joe Ledley goal early in the first-half. The game also marked Neil Lennon's 100th as Celtic manager, and the only goal came on 17 minutes. James Forrest raced down the right wing and his precise cutback was swept home at the far post by Ledley for his seventh goal of the season. There was controversy in the second-half when Daniel Majstorovic was red-carded for a last-man foul on Johnny Hayes, though that was later rescinded on appeal. And Inverness were also reduced to 10 men late in the game when Steve Williams was sent off.

Man of the Match:
Georgios Samaras

Story of the Season: Inverness Caledonian Thistle

September 24, 2011
Celtic 2-0 Inverness CT
(Ledley, Forrest)

Having returned from a midweek trip to the Highlands where they had knocked Ross County out of the Scottish Cup, Celtic played host to County's local rivals, Inverness Caley Thistle, in an SPL game. And first-half goals from Joe Ledley and James Forrest gave Neil Lennon's side a comfortable 2-0 lead. The opening goal came in the 28th minute. Beram Kayal found Ledley with a low pass and the midfielder took one touch before rifling a low shot past Ryan Esson from 25 yards. Five minutes later, Celtic doubled their advantage. From a swift breakaway, Ki delivered a perfectly-weight pass through the middle for James Forrest and the young winger confidently swept the bouncing ball into the corner.

Man of the Match: Joe Ledley

November 19, 2011
Inverness CT 0-2 Celtic
(Stokes 2)

Anthony Stokes was the goal hero in the Highlands with a double as Celtic overcame 10-man Inverness Caley Thistle to win 2-0. While Greg Tansey was red-carded in the first-half, it took until the hour mark before the Hoops made the breakthrough. Great combination play on the edge of the box between James Forrest and Gary Hooper saw the Englishman slid the ball along the six-yard box for Stokes to finish off a great move. And though the Irishman was denied a second goal just a few minutes later when Ryan Esson saved well from a shot, he soon made it 2-0. Again, James Forrest was involved, and while his shot was blocked, the rebound fell invitingly for Stokes who volleyed home.

Man of the Match:
Anthony Stokes

HOOPS' POINT TO PROVE

October 15, 2011
Kilmarnock 3-3 Celtic
(Stokes 2, Mulgrew)

A game that could have heralded the effective end of Celtic's season ended up being the starting point for a remarkable recovery that culminated in the SPL title returning to Paradise. The first 45 minutes at Rugby Park could only be described as disastrous for the Hoops as they conceded three goals without reply, as Dean Shiels, Paul Heffernan and James Fowler all netted for the home side. As the teams trooped off at the break, the only question appeared to be how many goals would Kilmarnock score? Whatever Neil Lennon said in the dressing room, however, and it was probably the team-talk of his fledgling managerial career, it was a different Celtic that emerged for the second-half. They battled and fought their way back into the game, with Anthony Stokes scoring two goals in the space of three minutes, the first a superb free-kick and the second a drive from 25 yards. And on 80 minutes, Charlie Mulgrew completed a remarkable comeback, bundling home the ball after Daniel Majstorovic had headed a free-kick towards goal.

Man of the Match: James Forrest

December 24, 2011
Celtic 2-1 Kilmarnock
(Samaras 2)

Celtic's victory over Kilmarnock on Christmas Eve was the perfect illustration of how Neil Lennon had turned his side's fortunes around. The 2-1 win, thanks to a Georgios Samaras double, coupled with Rangers' defeat against St Mirren, meant that the Hoops would go top of the league if they won the derby match a few days later. From a side that had looked dead and buried at Rugby Park back in October, to one that was already showing real signs that they could be champions, it was a remarkable transformation. The goals on Christmas Eve came either side of half-time. Cha raced to the byline before crossing into the penalty area and Samaras rose above Mohamadou Sissoko to head the ball home. And on 53 minutes, the Greek striker scored again. Picking up Hooper's short pass at the edge of the 18-yard box, the striker controlled the ball before slamming it home with a powerful left-foot shot. Killie scored a late goal from Danny Racchi, but the Hoops held on for a vital win.

Man of the Match:
Georgios Samaras

April 7, 2012
Kilmarnock 0-6 Celtic
(Mulgrew 2, Hooper 2, Loovens, Ledley)

CELTIC were crowned Champions at Rugby Park with an outstanding 6-0 victory against Kilmarnock, securing the first title triumph under Neil Lennon. The emphatic victory was completed by a stylish performance in front of 14,000 travelling Celtic supporters in Ayrshire, thanks to two goals from Charlie Mulgrew and a double from Gary Hooper along with strikes from Glenn Loovens and Joe Ledley. On an afternoon when everyone in a Celtic jersey was superb, Mulgrew still managed to capture the Man of the Match award with two goals and two assists in a blistering first 45 minutes which ensured that it was just a matter of counting down the second-half minutes until the referee's whistle signalled that Celtic were the champions. The Hoops had done it with style and panache and are worthy and well-deserved champions.

Man of the Match:
Charlie Mulgrew

CELTS IN STATS

OCTOBER 15, 2011
KILMARNOCK 3-3 CELTIC
(STOKES 2, MULGREW)

KILMARNOCK (4-4-2): Jaakkola; Pursehouse, Buijs, Sissoko, McKeown; Fowler, Pascali, Kelly, Shiels; Harkins, Heffernan. Not Used: Letheren, Hay, Silva, Dayton, Kroca, Fisher, Kennedy.

CELTIC (4-4-2): Forster; Cha (El Kaddouri 68) Majstorovic, Mulgrew, Matthews; Forrest, Ki, Kayal (Wanyama 45) Ledley; Hooper (Bangura 45) Stokes. Not Used: Zaluska, M Wilson, Rogne, Loovens.

MATCH STATS

Kilmarnock		Celtic
45	Possession	55
7	Shots on Target	8
4	Shots off Target	6
14	Fouls (conceded)	10
3	Corners	2
3	Yellow cards	3
0	Red cards	0

DECEMBER 24, 2011
CELTIC 2-1 KILMARNOCK
(SAMARAS 2)

CELTIC (4-4-2) Forster; Cha, Mulgrew, Wanyama; Ledley; Forrest (K. Wilson 49), Brown, Kayal, Ki (Rogne 90); Hooper, Samaras (Bangura 66). Not used: Zaluska, Izaguirre, McCourt, McGeouch.

KILMARNOCK (4-4-2): Bell; Fowler, Sissoko, Pascali, McKeown; Kelly, Buijs (Dayton 62), Shiels (Racchi 72), Hay (Kennedy 78); Harkins, Heffernan. Not used: Jaakkola, Kroca, Pursehouse, Fisher.

MATCH STATS

Celtic		Kilmarnock
53	Possession	47
4	Shots on Target	2
6	Shots off Target	3
12	Fouls (conceded)	14
8	Corners	2
1	Yellow cards	2
0	Red cards	0

APRIL 7, 2012
KILMARNOCK 0-6 CELTIC
(MULGREW 2, HOOPER 2, LOOVENS, LEDLEY)

KILMARNOCK (4-4-2): Bell; Gordon (Barbour 46), Nelson, Sissoko, Johnston; Hay (Dayton 46), Fowler, Kelly, Harkins; Van Tornhout (Heffernan 61), Shiels. Not used: Letheren, Racchi, Pursehouse, Kennedy.

CELTIC (4-4-2) Forster; Matthews, Loovens, K Wilson, Mulgrew (Blackman 76); Brown (F Twardzik 48), Ki, Ledley, Commons; Samaras (Stokes 74), Hooper. Not used: Zaluska, Cha, Brozek, Ibrahim.

MATCH STATS

Kilmarnock		Celtic
45	Possession	55
2	Shots on Target	9
2	Shots off Target	3
9	Fouls (conceded)	9
2	Corners	8
3	Yellow cards	1
0	Red cards	0

V

Celts keep winning Well

September 10, 2011
Celtic 4-0 Motherwell
(Forrest 2, Ledley, Ki)

Celtic recorded a comprehensive 4-0 victory over Motherwell in the first meeting of the season between the sides. The game also saw debuts for Mo Bangura and on-loan defender Badr El Kaddouri. The Hoops opened the scoring after just nine minutes when James Forrest finished off a great move involving Anthony Stokes and Gary Hooper. And the young Scot would complete the scoring on 74 minutes with a shot from the edge of the box. In between those two goals, Joe Ledley and Ki Sung Yueng also netted for Celtic. Ledley's goal came on 33 minutes, with Stokes again having a hand in the move, and Ki Sung Yueng made it 3-0 on 67 minutes when he slammed home the ball from 20 yards out.

Man of the Match: James Forrest

November 6, 2011
Motherwell 1-2 Celtic
(Stokes, Hooper)

Celtic went into the game at Fir Park back in November 15 points behind then league leaders Rangers, and the 2-1 victory was one of the most important wins of the season for the Hoops. Michael Higdon had given the home side the lead on 11 minutes when he headed home beyond Fraser Forster, but that goal was cancelled out three minutes later. Georgios Samaras got on the head of a Kris Commons corner, and the ball fell to Anthony Stokes, who finished well. The winning goal came with 10 minutes of the match remaining, when, following good work from Paddy McCourt, Stokes fired the ball into the six-yard box for substitute Gary Hooper to bundle it home.

Man of the Match:
Anthony Stokes

February 25, 2012
Celtic 1-0 Motherwell
(Hooper)

A tight game at Celtic Park between the league leaders and the side chasing second-spot in the SPL was decided by a solitary Gary Hooper goal on the hour mark. The striker took his tally to 20 goals for the season as Celtic made it 20 consecutive wins in all three domestic competitions, including 17 in the SPL. It was a run which began when they last faced Motherwell at the start of November. The only goal of the game came from an Adam Matthews throw-in. Georgios Samaras chested it into the path of Hooper who blasted it into the net from six yards out to give Neil Lennon's side another important three points in their quest for the title.

Man of the Match:
Thomas Rogne

CELTS IN STATS

SEPTEMBER 10, 2011
CELTIC 4-0 MOTHERWELL
(FORREST 2, LEDLEY, KI)

CELTIC (4-4-2): Forster; Matthews, K Wilson, Mulgrew, El Kaddouri; Forrest, Ki, Kayal (Wanyama 82), Ledley (Commons 70); Stokes (Bangura 67), Hooper. Not used: Zaluska, M Wilson, Loovens, Samaras.

MOTHERWELL (4-5-1): Randolph; Hammell, Craigan, Clancy, Hutchinson (Humphrey 30); Law, Jennings, Hately, Lasley, Murphy; Higdon. Not used: Hollis, McHugh, Forbes, Page, Halsman, Carswell.

MATCH STATS

Celtic		Motherwell
63	Possession	37
8	Shots on Target	1
8	Shots off Target	3
10	Fouls (conceded)	8
6	Corners	8
1	Yellow cards	2
0	Red cards	0

NOVEMBER 6, 2011
MOTHERWELL 1-2 CELTIC
(STOKES, HOOPER)

MOTHERWELL (4-5-1): Randolph; Hately, Clancy, Craigan, Hammell; Humphrey (Daley 80), Lasley, Jennings (Carswell 73), Law, Murphy (Hutchinson 80); Higdon. Not used: Bradley, Forbes, Smith, Page.

CELTIC (4-2-3-1): Forster; Cha, Majstorovic, Rogne, Matthews; Wanyama, Kayal; Forrest (McGeouch 89), Commons (Hooper 62), Samaras (McCourt 76); Stokes. Not used: Zaluska, Chalmers, Fraser, McGregor.

MATCH STATS

Motherwell		Celtic
46	Possession	54
3	Shots on Target	4
1	Shots off Target	1
20	Fouls (conceded)	8
11	Corners	2
2	Yellow cards	1
1	Red cards	0

FEBRUARY 25, 2012
CELTIC 1-0 MOTHERWELL
(HOOPER)

CELTIC (4-4-2): Forster; Matthews, K Wilson, Rogne, Mulgrew; Forrest (Commons 88), Wanyama (Stokes 59), Ki, Ledley; Hooper (Cha 76), Samaras. Not used: Zaluska, Majstorovic, Brozek, Izaguirre.

MOTHERWELL (4-4-2): Randolph; Hateley, Hutchinson, Clancy, Hammell; Murphy (Humphrey 63), Lasley, Jennings, Law; Higdon, Ojamaa (Daley 79). Not used: Bradley, Craigan, Forbes, Page, Carswell.

MATCH STATS

Celtic		Motherwell
51	Possession	49
7	Shots on Target	1
5	Shots off Target	1
10	Fouls (conceded)	20
9	Corners	2
1	Yellow cards	4
0	Red cards	0

V

DERBY DAZE AT PARADISE

December 28, 2011
Celtic 1-0 Rangers
(Ledley)

The last game of 2011 saw Celtic beat Rangers 1-0, courtesy of a Joe Ledley goal. Just as importantly, the victory saw the Hoops return to the top of the SPL table. It represented a remarkable turnaround in fortunes for Neil Lennon's side, who had been 15 points behind their city rivals at the beginning of November. Now, going into the new year, Celtic were back on top of the table, and it was a position they would not relinquish for the rest of the season. The only goal of the game came on 52 minutes when Ledley rose high above everyone else in the box to head home a Charlie Mulgrew corner.

Man of the Match: Thomas Rogne

September 18, 2011
Rangers 4-2 Celtic
(Hooper, El Kaddouri)

Celtic lost the first derby of the season 4-2 as Rangers came from behind to secure all three points at Ibrox. Steven Naismith put the home side ahead, but the Hoops fought back well. Gary Hooper scored a superb equaliser before on-loan defender, Badr El Kaddouri put Celtic ahead with a shot from outside the box. It was a fortuitous goal, which relied on Allan McGregor fumbling the ball into the net. But having taken a half-time lead, the Hoops were second-best after the break and conceded three goals. And to make matters worse, Charlie Mulgrew was sent off after collecting his second yellow card of the match.

Man of the Match:
Gary Hooper

March 25, 2012
Rangers 3-2 Celtic
(Brown, Rogne)

Celtic travelled to Ibrox knowing that three points would secure the SPL title. But in a controversial derby match, they were reduced to nine men, had Neil Lennon sent from the dugout at half-time, and lost the match 3-2. At one point, the Hoops were trailing 3-0 but the nine men bravely fought back and scored two late goals, from a Scott Brown penalty and a Thomas Rogne header. Rangers had taken an early lead before Cha Du-Ri was harshly sent off. He was followed in the second-half by Victor Wanyama, by which time the manager was watching the game in the Ibrox media room, having been sent off at the break, and security fears preventing him from sitting in the Main Stand at Ibrox. The defeat, however, merely delayed the inevitable title celebrations at Paradise.

Man of the Match:
Scott Brown

SEPTEMBER 18, 2011
RANGERS 4-2 CELTIC
(HOOPER, EL KADDOURI)

RANGERS (4-4-2) McGregor; Whittaker, Goian, Bocanegra, Papac; Naismith, Davis, Edu, Wylde; Lafferty (McCulloch 81) Jelavic (Healy 90). Not Used: Alexander, Broadfoot, Fleck, Ortiz, Perry.

CELTIC (4-4-2) Forster; M Wilson, K Wilson, Loovens, El Kaddouri (Stokes 63); Brown (Forrest 75) Ki, Kayal, Mulgrew; Samaras (Bangura 83) Hooper. Not Used: Zaluska, Matthews, Wanyama, Ledley.

MATCH STATS

Rangers		Celtic
53	Possession	47
6	Shots on Target	5
7	Shots off Target	1
8	Fouls (conceded)	19
3	Corners	3
0	Yellow cards	2
0	Red cards	1

DECEMBER 28, 2011
CELTIC 1-0 RANGERS
(LEDLEY)

CELTIC (4-4-2) Forster; Matthews, Rogne, Mulgrew, Ledley; Brown, Kayal, (Ki 77), Wanyama; Forrest; Hooper (Stokes 86), Samaras. Not Used: Zaluska, Cha, Bangura, K Wilson, McCourt.

RANGERS (4-4-2) McGregor; Broadfoot, Bartley, Bocanegra, Papac; Aluko (Wylde 67) Davis, McCulloch (Healy 79) Wallace (Edu 79); Lafferty, Jelavic. Not Used: Alexander, Weir, Fleck, Bendikson.

MATCH STATS

Celtic		Rangers
56	Possession	44
9	Shots on Target	2
5	Shots off Target	4
11	Fouls (conceded)	22
7	Corners	4
1	Yellow cards	3
0	Red cards	0

MARCH 25, 2012
RANGERS 3-2 CELTIC
(BROWN, ROGNE)

RANGERS (4-4-2): McGregor; Whittaker, Goian, Bocanegra, Wallace (Kerkar 78); Aluko (Little 71), Davis, Edu, McCulloch, Papac, McCabe (Lafferty 60). Not used: Alexander, Bedoya, Perry, Mitchell.

CELTIC (4-4-2): Forster; Cha, Rogne, Mulgrew, Matthews; Brown, Wanyama, Ki (Commons 70), Ledley, Samaras; Stokes (Izaguirre 29). Not used: Zaluska, K. Wilson, McGeouch, Hooper, Brozek.

MATCH STATS

Rangers		Celtic
52	Possession	48
11	Shots on Target	3
6	Shots off Target	4
19	Fouls (conceded)	14
6	Corners	4
1	Yellow cards	0
1	Red cards	2

V

Match Point Celtic

April 1, 2012
Celtic 2-0 St Johnstone
(Samaras, Millar og)

Celtic moved to within a point of securing the 2011/12 SPL title with a 2-0 win over St Johnstone. It was a hard-fought victory against a side that had won at Celtic Park earlier in the season, and who had climbed as high as fourth in the table. And Neil Lennon's side had to wait until the 66th minute before they got the vital breakthrough. Kris Commons fired in a free-kick and Georgios Samaras rose high above the defence to head home. And the Greek striker set up Celtic's second just four minutes later, driving down the right flank and delivering a cross into the six-yard box which Chris Millar turned into his own net.

Man of the Match: Georgios Samaras

December 18, 2011
St Johnstone 0-2 Celtic
(Hooper, Ki)

Celtic made it a magnificent seven domestic wins on the spin, cutting the gap at the top of the SPL back to four points, with a dominant 2-0 victory over St Johnstone at McDiarmid Park. After some incessant pressure, Gary Hooper deservedly put Neil Lennon's men ahead on the hour mark with his 15th goal of the campaign. Four minutes later, Ki sealed the points, finishing from close-range after an incisive counter-attack. The only negative in an otherwise impressive afternoon was the fractured cheekbone suffered by defender Daniel Majstorovic following an accidental clash with St Johnstone player David Robertson. The injury would rule the Swedish defender out of action for the next couple of months.

Man of the Match:
Georgios Samaras

CELTS IN STATS

AUGUST 21, 2011
CELTIC 0-1 ST JOHNSTONE

CELTIC (4-4-2) Forster; Matthews, Majstorovic, Wanyama, Mulgrew (Wilson 45); Brown, Ki, Ledley (Forrest 74), Commons (McCourt 61); Maloney, Stokes. Not Used: Zaluska, Samaras, Cha, Murphy.

ST JOHNSTONE (4-4-2) Enckelman; Mackay, Maybury, McCracken, Wright, Craig; Morris, M Davidson, C. Davidson; Sheridan (Higgins 63) Sandaza (Haber 72). Not Used: Mannus, Adams, Moffat, May, Caddis.

MATCH STATS

Celtic		St Johnstone
63	Possession	37
7	Shots on Target	3
10	Shots off Target	2
8	Fouls (conceded)	6
9	Corners	7
0	Yellow cards	3
0	Red cards	0

DECEMBER 18, 2011
ST JOHNSTONE 0-2 CELTIC
(HOOPER, KI)

CELTIC (4-3-3) Forster; Cha, Majstorovic (Rogne 33) Wanyama, Mulgrew; Brown, Kayal (McGeouch 77) Ki; Forrest, Hooper (Bangura 82), Samaras. Not Used: Zaluska, Wilson, Blackman, F. Twardzik.

ST JOHNSTONE (4-5-1) Enckelman; Mackay, Anderson, McCracken, Maybury; Millar, Moon, Davidson, Craig (Gibson 80); Robertson (Finnigan 39); Haber. Not Used: Mannus, Parkin, Duman, McIntosh, Gray.

MATCH STATS

St Johnstone		Celtic
36	Possession	64
3	Shots on Target	11
1	Shots off Target	7
13	Fouls (conceded)	6
3	Corners	6
3	Yellow cards	1
0	Red cards	0

August 21, 2011
Celtic 0-1 St Johnstone

Despite dominating in terms of possession and chances created, Celtic unexpectedly lost 1-0 at home to St Johnstone. The only goal of the game came on the hour mark when Saints' defender Dave Mackay netted from an acute angle. By that point, the Hoops had squandered a number of opportunities to score. In the first few minutes, they were awarded a penalty after Anthony Stokes was brought down, but Kris Commons failed to convert the spot-kick. Commons also struck the post from a free-kick, while the woodwork would also deny Paddy McCourt. And some resolute defending from St Johnstone ensured an unlikely three points for the visitors.

Man of the Match: Anthony Stokes

APRIL 1, 2012
CELTIC 2-0 ST JOHNSTONE
(SAMARAS, MILLAR og)

CELTIC (4-4-2) Forster; Lustig (Matthews 55), Rogne, Loovens, Mulgrew; Commons, Brown, Ledley, Samaras; Stokes (Ki 63), Hooper (Blackman 87). Not Used: Zaluska, Izaguirre, K Wilson, McGeouch.

ST JOHNSTONE (4-4-2) Mannus; Mackay, McCracken, Wright, Maybury; Croft (Oyenuga 90) Millar, Morris (Moon 85) Craig; Sandaza, Sheridan. Not Used: Enckelman, Anderson, Robertson, Moffat, Mitchell.

MATCH STATS

Celtic		St Johnstone
59	Possession	41
8	Shots on Target	0
6	Shots off Target	4
4	Fouls (conceded)	11
4	Corners	7
0	Yellow cards	3
0	Red cards	0

August 28, 2011
St Mirren 0-2 Celtic
(Hooper 2)

There aren't many SPL teams who enjoy the majority of possession against Celtic and, indeed, there have only been three league games where that has been the case this season. Two of those matches came at Ibrox, while the other match was the first meeting between the Hoops and St Mirren. Danny Lennon's side had more of the ball throughout the match, but it was Neil Lennon's side who did more with their possession, and left Paisley in possession of all three points. Both goals came from Gary Hooper inside the first 12 minutes. Playing a one-two with Anthony Stokes, Hooper coolly slotted it into the net, and a few minutes later, Hooper pounced on a slack pass from Paul McGowan to make it 2-0.

Man of the Match: James Forrest

SAINTS & WINNERS

November 26, 2011
Celtic 5-0 St Mirren
(Samaras, Hooper 3, McGeouch)

Celtic enjoyed a comfortable 5-0 victory over St Mirren, with Gary Hooper netting a hat-trick and teenager Dylan McGeouch scoring a candidate for goal of the season with a wonderful solo effort. Georgios Samaras gave Celtic the lead on four minutes, and just four minutes later Hooper scored the first of his goals. The Englishman added two more after the break as Neil Lennon's side pressed home their superiority, and the 4-0 cushion allowed the manager to introduce 18-year-old McGeouch to proceedings. And the youngster had Paradise in raptures with an incredible goal. Picking the ball up on the edge of his own area, McGeouch went on a mazy run, evading several challenges before slotting the ball home from the edge of the St Mirren box.

Man of the Match: Gary Hooper

January 21, 2012
St Mirren 0-2 Celtic
(Forrest, Brown)

Paisley in January could never be described as picturesque, but it was a particularly bleak afternoon when Celtic visited St Mirren Park. While the Hoops were the stronger side throughout the afternoon it took until the 71st minute before they made the breakthrough. A corner was headed out to the edge of the box and Scott Brown's lay-off into the path of James Forrest saw the young Celt fire the ball home to give the Hoops the lead. And with two minutes of the match remaining, the Celtic captain made it 2-0. Gathering a short corner from Kris Commons, he controlled the ball and fired in an exquisite left-foot shot beyond the St Mirren goalkeeper, with the customary 'Broony' celebration following, much to the delight of the travelling Celtic support.

**Man of the Match:
Scott Brown**

GLASGOW CELTIC CHAMPIONS 2012

Jock Stein: 1965/66

IT is rightly acknowledged as the golden era in Celtic's history, and Jock Stein's reign was indeed a momentous one. The arrival of the former Hoops defender to take over as manager from Jimmy McGrory in 1965 was a pivotal moment and changed forever the club and its fortunes. From having been mired in post-war doldrums which had lasted for 20 years, suddenly Celtic became the dominant force in Scottish football, while they also bestrode the European stage, winning the European Cup in 1967 and reaching another final three years later.

Stein had cut his managerial teeth with Dunfermline, where he won the Scottish Cup in 1961 with a replay victory over Celtic, and from there he moved on to Hibernian. But his former club came calling and he officially took charge in March 1965. Less than two months later, the Hoops won the Scottish Cup, their first trophy success since 1957. It was a triumph celebrated by the long-suffering Celtic support, and it heralded the beginning of an incredible period of success.

The first of what would become an historic nine league titles in a row came in Stein's first full season in charge at Celtic Park, when his team finished two points clear of second-place Rangers. They would score 106 league goals that season, with Joe McBride top scorer with 31 in the league, and there was also a momentous 5-1 derby victory over Rangers on January 3, with Stevie Chalmers scoring a hat-trick.

The title wasn't absolutely secured until the last day of the season, and it took a Bobby Lennox goal in the final minute of that game at Fir Park to give Celtic a 1-0 win over Motherwell and, more importantly, to confirm them as Scottish champions for the first time since 1954.

That season, Celtic would also win the League Cup with a 2-1 victory over Rangers, and they narrowly missed out on a treble when they lost the Scottish Cup final to the Ibrox club in a replay. And the Hoops were also unlucky not to reach the final of the European Cup-Winners' Cup, getting knocked out of the semi-final 2-1 on aggregate by Liverpool. Twelve months later, they would make amends by lifting the 'Big Cup' in Lisbon.

JOCK STEIN HONOURS

League Championships (10)
1965/66, 1966/67, 1967/68, 1968/69, 1969/70,
1970/71, 1971/72, 1972/73, 1973/74, 1976/77

Scottish Cups (8)
1965, 1967, 1969, 1971, 1972, 1974, 1975, 1977

League Cup (6)
1965/66, 1966/67, 1967/68, 1968/69, 1969/70, 1974/75

European Cup
1967

SCOTTISH LEAGUE DIVISION ONE 1965/66

	PLD	W	D	L	F	A	PTS
CELTIC	34	27	3	4	106	30	57
Rangers	34	25	5	4	91	29	55
Kilmarnock	34	20	5	9	73	46	45
Dunfermline	34	19	6	9	94	55	44
Dundee Utd	34	19	5	10	79	51	43
Hibernian	34	16	6	12	81	55	38
Hearts	34	13	12	9	56	48	38
Aberdeen	34	15	6	13	61	54	36
Dundee	34	14	6	14	61	61	34
Falkirk	34	15	1	18	48	72	31
Clyde	34	13	4	17	62	64	30
Partick Thistle	34	10	10	14	55	64	30
Motherwell	34	12	4	18	52	69	28
St Johnstone	34	9	8	17	58	81	26
Stirling Albion	34	9	8	17	40	68	26
St Mirren	34	9	4	21	44	82	22
Morton	34	8	5	21	42	84	21
Hamilton	34	3	2	29	27	117	8

Billy McNeill: 1978/79

IT could be argued that Billy McNeill deserves two separate features on his 'first' title, since he won the league in 1978/79 in his debut season as Celtic manager, and then also secured the title when he returned for a second spell in charge for the club's centenary season. Both successes are ones which continue to be remembered and celebrated, and the man known as 'Cesar' was a pivotal figure in the triumphs.

McNeill had enjoyed incredible success as Jock Stein's captain, and he played 790 times for the Hoops, more than any other player in the club's history. Having left in 1975, he had short spells as manager of Clyde and then Aberdeen before returning to Paradise in 1978. It had seemed at the time unthinkable that Jock Stein would ever leave Celtic, but that's what happened after a trophy-less season in 1977/78 – the only time in his career as Celtic boss. The infamous picture of Stein and McNeill shaking hands either side of then chairman Desmond White seemed to capture perfectly the strained and less than amicable handing of the managerial reigns.

The first season in charge for McNeill saw him bring in some new faces who would prove vital in the club's future success, such as Davie Provan and Murdo MacLeod. And it was also a season when, due to a severe winter, Celtic didn't play a league game from December 23 to March 3. It meant that there was a hectic fixture schedule towards the end of the campaign, though it all eventually boiled down to Celtic's last game of the season when they played host to Rangers on Monday, May 21, 1979.

The game will be forever remembered in Celtic history books as the night '10 Men Won The League'. The Hoops had to do it the hard way, with Johnny Doyle red-carded early in the proceedings. Rangers only needed a draw, but Celtic produced an inspirational performance to win 4-2, with Murdo MacLeod's late goal the icing on the cake as the Hoops celebrated a momentous title triumph.

McNeill, of course, famously returned to Celtic for a second spell as manager in 1987, and duly delivered a Centenary double for the club.

BILLY McNEILL HONOURS

League Championships (4)
1978/79, 1980/81, 1981/82, 1987/88

Scottish Cups (3)
1980, 1988, 1989

League Cup (1)
1982/83

SCOTTISH PREMIER DIVISION 1978/79

	PLD	W	D	L	F	A	PTS
CELTIC	36	21	6	9	61	37	48
Rangers	36	18	9	9	52	35	45
Dundee Utd	36	18	8	10	56	37	44
Aberdeen	36	13	14	9	59	36	40
Hibernian	36	12	13	11	44	48	37
St Mirren	36	15	6	15	45	41	36
Morton	36	12	12	12	52	53	36
Partick Thistle	36	13	8	15	42	39	34
Hearts	36	8	7	21	39	71	23
Motherwell	36	5	7	24	33	86	17

10 TOP GOALS WHICH DECIDED THE TITLE

Gary Hooper v Rangers
Ibrox
September 18, 2011

Gary Hooper provided an exquisite goal in the first derby clash of the season at Ibrox to cancel out an early opener from the home side. The goal was made by Scott Brown's superb reverse pass from the inside-left position, which deceived the entire Rangers defence and found its way to Hooper. Controlling the ball superbly on the right-hand side of the penalty area, about 12 yards out, the Englishman hit a low, spinning shot beyond Allan McGregor and into the far corner of the net, to the delight of the Celtic fans in the Broomloan Road Stand.

Ki Sung Yueng v Motherwell
Celtic Park
September 10, 2011

Ki Sung Yueng's superb goal on 67 minutes completed a 4-0 rout of Motherwell at Celtic Park. Gary Hooper gathered the ball in the opposition half and cut inside from the right, surging forward towards goal. He played the ball to Joe Ledley on the edge of the box, who knocked it back, first-time, into the path of Ki. And the Korean midfielder hit a sweet shot with the outside of his right foot from 25 yards out that sailed into the top left-hand corner of the net, beyond the reach of the diving Darren Randolph in the Motherwell goal.

Anthony Stokes v Kilmarnock
Rugby Park
October 15, 2011

Trailing 3-0 at half-time, Anthony Stokes' free-kick on 73 minutes sparked a remarkable comeback at Rugby Park for the Hoops. The award came after James Forrest, who was exceptional throughout the game, was fouled 25 yards from goal, and Stokes stepped up to fire an unstoppable shot into the back of the Kilmarnock net, much to the delight, and relief, of the strong travelling support. Three minutes later, the Irishman scored again, this time with a powerful shot from outside the box and Celtic were on their way to an unlikely, but very welcome point.

Dylan McGeouch v St Mirren
Celtic Park
November 26, 2011

In only his second substitute appearance for Celtic, Dylan McGeouch scored a wonder goal that had the whole of Paradise on their feet, on a day when the Hoops hit five past St Mirren without reply. The 18-year-old's goal was the last, and the pick of the bunch, and came on 72 minutes. He won the ball on the edge of the Celtic penalty area and set off on a mazy run, first evading Jim Goodwin and then surging towards goal. He had options either side to pass but the young Celt kept going towards goal, cutting into the box and firing beyond three St Mirren defenders and into the net.

Anthony Stokes v Dunfermline
East End Park
January 2, 2012

Celtic, now SPL league leaders at the start of 2012, visited East End Park for the first fixture of the new year. And a comfortable 3-0 win for the Hoops got underway with a tremendous Anthony Stokes goal after just 18 minutes. Charlie Mulgrew played a short corner with James Forrest before firing a left-foot cross from the right-hand side into the Dunfermline penalty area. Samaras' backwards header at the far post landed at the feet of Anthony Stokes on the edge of the penalty area, and the Irishman executed a precise right-foot curler into the top left-hand corner of the Dunfermline net.

Victor Wanyama v Hearts
Celtic Park
December 10, 2011

Victor Wanyama opened his scoring account for Celtic in spectacular style, netting the only goal of the game against Hearts at Celtic Park. The goal which broke the deadlock in a tight match came on 72 minutes. Scott Brown knocked the ball back to Charlie Mulgrew who flicked it forward, first-time, to Wanyama. And from 25 yards out, the young Kenyan internationalist unleashed a powerful right-foot shot which rocketed into the top, left-hand corner of the net, giving Marian Kello in the Hearts goal absolutely no chance. The goal was enough to keep Celtic's impressive winning run going.

Scott Brown v St Mirren
St Mirren Park
January 21, 2012

It was, to say the least, a dreich day at St Mirren Park when Celtic visited back in January. But goals from James Forrest and Scott Brown sealed a 2-0 win for Neil Lennon's men. Brown, who had set up Forrest for the opener, completed the scoring on 88 minutes. He gathered a short corner from Kris Commons on the edge of the box, and moving the ball on to his left foot, the Celtic skipper curled an unstoppable shot into the St Mirren net for his first goal of the season followed, much to the delight of the drenched Celtic support, by the customary 'Broony' celebration.

Gary Hooper v Hibernian
Easter Road
February 19, 2012

This was a classic counter-attacking goal from Celtic as they put Hibernian to the sword. And it was great combination play from Anthony Stokes and Gary Hooper which created the goal, with the Englishman providing the finishing touch. Victor Wanyama won the ball 30 yards from the Celtic goal, knocking it forward to Hooper. And from the edge of the centre-circle, he knocked it out to Stokes on the left-hand side of the pitch. Hooper continued his run as Stokes surged forward, cutting inside and supplying a great pass to his strike partner who, from the edge of the six-yard box, fired a low shot into the net.

Charlie Mulgrew v Kilmarnock
Rugby Park
April 7, 2012

Charlie Mulgrew produced a Man of the Match performance as Celtic sealed the title in style at Rugby Park. He scored two and set up two goals in a blistering first-half. The pick of the goals was Mulgrew's second and Celtic's third, which came on 35 minutes. He gathered the ball on the left-hand side of the pitch, cut inside and from the edge of the box, curled a superb low right-foot shot into the far corner beyond Cammy Bell in the Kilmarnock goal.

Charlie Mulgrew v Dunfermline
Celtic Park
February 22, 2012

It was top versus bottom at Celtic Park, but it was a tough night for the Hoops, who eventually won the match 2-0. And it was Charlie Mulgrew who opened the scoring just after the half-hour mark. Ki Sung Yueng knocked a pass inside to Mulgrew, who gathered the ball on the edge of the centre-circle in the Dunfermline half of the field. And, striding forward, the defender unleashed a ferocious left-foot shot from nearly 40 yards out which rocketed into the Dunfermline net, beyond the despairing dive of Pars keeper, Chris Smith.

AND ONE VITAL SAVE...

Fraser Forster v Hearts
Celtic Park
December 10, 2011

As Celtic were building up an impressive run of league wins and eating into Rangers' lead at the top of the SPL, they faced a tough and resilient Hearts side at Celtic Park in the middle of December. Victor Wanyama had given the Hoops a 1-0 lead with a spectacular shot on 72 minutes but late in the game, referee Calum Murray adjudged the Kenyan midfielder to have handled the ball inside the box and awarded Hearts a penalty. Eggert Jonsson stepped up but Celtic goalkeeper, Fraser Forster, produced an outstanding save to ensure Neil Lennon's side won all three points. It was a vital stop from the impressive Englishman and a pivotal moment in Celtic's successful campaign to reclaim the SPL title.

CHARLIE'S A BHOY TO BE PROUD OF

WHILE it was an outstanding team performance to clinch the title against Kilmarnock, it was Charlie Mulgrew who was instrumental in the wonderful display of football.

Scoring two goals, setting up another two and putting in a typically strong performance, the defender was Man of the Match in the 6-0 victory.

"We started well as a team at a high tempo and Kilmarnock couldn't handle us," Mulgrew said. "I was lucky enough to score the first goal and it got us off to a great start. I was happy with my performance but the main thing was we won the game, and it didn't matter how we did that, but we did it in style, which was even better.

"You could see the intensity we played at, it was very high, right from the first whistle, and if we play like that we will cause teams a lot of bother. I think the way we started the game, Kilmarnock didn't know what to do.

We got that early goal and it relaxed us."

Mulgrew rejoined the club last season and has been, over the past 18 months, once of Celtic's most consistent performers. As well as being in the running for Player of the Year, he was also rewarded with his first Scotland cap.

"I owe a lot to the manager and the coaching staff for bringing me back here and I can't thank them enough," he said. "They've shown a good belief in me and it's given me confidence. I'm happy with the way things are going and it's great to win my first title.

"I always believed in myself. I knew it would take a wee bit to settle even though I'd been here before, but it was different coaching staff and different players so I knew it would take time. I kept working away and thankfully it's worked out for me."

While he has enjoyed great success on the field this season, Mulgrew also had to cope

with the heartbreaking loss of his dad, who passed away in November. And clinching the title has been an emotional time for the player and his family.

"It's very humbling to hear the reception I get from the fans," he said. "Growing up as a Celtic fan myself I never imagined they would be singing my name one day. Even when things weren't going great with my dad they were great with me and I can't thank them enough.

"It was hard at the time. Anybody who's had that kind of loss knows the feeling and how difficult it can be. But it's about having the mental strength and doing what he would have wanted me to do.

"I know he would have wanted me to get on with football and concentrate on the job, so once I had time to think about things, I got back into it and it was total focus from there on in. He's always in my mind, of course, and it gives me an extra bit of motivation."

"WE'VE been waiting for this for quite a long time, so to finally cross the line is a great feeling. All the boys and the fans just wanted to get the title done and the performance was brilliant on Saturday. To do that in such an important game was incredible.

"The game was one of the best we have played all year so to do that in such a massive game was fantastic. It was a bit nervous before the start especially with me in the stands but the boys were great and hopefully we can keep this going now and finish the season well.

"The turning point is hard to say, but it might have been at the same stadium we won the league - the 3-3 game. So it was good to win the league there was great.

"The supporters? All I can say about the fans on Saturday was that we played at home. That's all I can say.

"Players go to Celtic as you want to win titles and compete in Europe, so for us to get this is massive. The fans have been waiting on this for a long time and so have we. It's a brilliant feeling.

"We want to get more but it's hard work – we know that. After enjoying this, we just have to look forward."

- THOMAS ROGNE

"THIS is why you play football – to win things and the ultimate prize is to win the league. We're delighted we've done it this year and we did it in some style. You could see from the deliveries, the defenders were willing to go for it and it was a real team performance. That sums up the club at the moment, we're a real team and we work hard for each other and it was all about winning the league.

"The fans were great but they're not just like that when we win things - when times are bad they are also still there and that shows they are real supporters through thick and thin.

"I struggled in the beginning with a lot of injuries and every time I was back in the team I would get injured again. Then when I got back to full fitness the team was on a run of about 20 games so it's hard to get back into that. You have to wait for your chance. You can't say to the manager, 'What about me?' So I waited for my chance and luckily I could play my part in the last few games.

"I got my goal and it was a great cross from Charlie, he whipped a good ball in and I went for it. I was free at the second post so I headed it across goal and it went in.

"We played well and it's good to help your team-mates out when they need it. It was a great team performance and I'm delighted we did it with a bit of style."

- GLENN LOOVENS

"IT'S up there and probably the best moment in my career. I'm a Nottingham Forest fan and won promotion with them so that was a proud moment but being champions is right up there.

"It means a lot to the players. I think everyone is just finally glad we have done it as I said, every week we need this title, and now to have done it by winning 6-0 and playing really well, everyone is delighted.

"Without a doubt I will dedicate it to my friend, Kevin Munn *(Kelvin's friend, Kevin Munn, was murdered three yeas ago in Nottingham, aged just 19).*

"He was a massive football fan and always came to see me when he wasn't playing himself. He wasn't a professional but he loved the game. He was only a young boy when he was murdered so he is always in my thoughts.

"It gives me goose pimples thinking about it just now. I keep in touch with his family and spoke to his dad the other day when I went back down south."

- KELVIN WILSON

Davie Hay: 1985/86

THE 1980s were strange years for Celtic in particular and Scottish football in general. The reason? The Hoops' main rivals for trophies weren't old traditional foes Rangers, but the threat came from the north east in the shape of Aberdeen and Dundee United and, indeed, such was their rise, it was not unknown for Celtic to be doing the chasing. However, in season 1985/86, another hat was thrown into the ring and it was maroon coloured as Hearts were flexing their championship credentials for the first time since season 1964/65, immediately prior to Celtic's historic nine-in-a-row.

That season the Tynecastle side lost to Kilmarnock on goal-average and this term, with Davie Hay at the helm in Celtic Park, Hearts were to miss out in similarly dramatic fashion as the Hoops took the final 90 minutes of the season by the scruff of the neck.

The campaign that resulted in Hay's first championship started in an equally tense scenario as Hearts led Celtic by 1-0 at Tynecastle thanks to a goal from former Hoop John Colquhoun until the final minute when Paul McStay equalised in off the post – nobody inside the ground realised just how important that goal would be at the end of the season.

Titles are, by their very nature, long and arduous affairs but every now and again everything completely hinges on one day and on this season that day was May 3, 1986 when Hay took his Celtic side to his hometown of Paisley while long-term frontrunners Hearts travelled north to play Dundee at Dens Park.

Hearts had 50 points with a goal-difference of +28 while Celtic had 48 points and a goal-difference of +24. In those days of two points for a win, if Hearts drew then the title was theirs no matter what happened while Celtic had to win to have any hope at all. The short story is that Celtic won 5-0 while Hearts lost 2-0 to a double from Dundee substitute Albert Kidd and Celtic won the title by three clear goals – if goal-difference had been used in 1965 instead of goal-average, Hearts would have won the title and the vice-versa scenario was the case in '86.

DAVIE HAY HONOURS

League Championships (1)
1985/86

Scottish Cups (1)
1985

SCOTTISH PREMIER DIVISION 1985/86

	PLD	W	D	L	F	A	PTS
CELTIC	**36**	**20**	**10**	**6**	**67**	**38**	**50**
Hearts	36	20	10	6	59	33	50
Dundee Utd	36	18	11	7	59	31	47
Aberdeen	36	16	12	8	62	31	44
Rangers	36	13	9	14	53	45	35
Dundee	36	14	7	15	45	51	35
St Mirren	36	13	6	18	42	63	31
Hibernian	36	11	6	19	49	63	28
Motherwell	36	7	6	23	33	66	20
Clydebank	36	6	8	22	29	77	20

Wim Jansen: 1997/98

OF the previous nine Celtic managers, only five had lifted the league title and of the four who didn't, only one hadn't previously played for the club. That somewhat exclusive club contained Liam Brady – a world-class footballer who had failed to convert his undoubted magic from the pitch to the backroom. That club was about to enrol a second member but while the Irishman was flung in at the deep end with Celtic being his first managerial job, Dutchman Wim Jansen was different – he had past hot-seat experience.

He didn't arrive in any old season, though, as he would **HAVE** to repeat the feat of previous incumbents Jock Stein and Billy McNeill by winning the title at the very first time of asking. The reason? Stein's astonishing record of nine-in-a-row was under threat from the south side of the city and Jansen **HAD** to succeed where the four previous managers had failed and wrest the title from Rangers' hands.

He drafted in new players – almost a full team and some such as Paul Lambert were to grace the club for years but such was Jansen's inside knowledge of Dutch football, particularly concerning the get-out clause of a Swedish striker at Feyenoord, that was not only to seal the destination of this season's title, but also tilt the course of Celtic's history.

Celtic got Henrik Larsson for a song and we've been singing his praises so much ever since it's a wonder Jansen wasn't charged with Grand Larssony such is the value of the striker to Celtic Football Club and its followers. With the League Cup already in the bag, the title came agonisingly down to the final day of the season after Celtic had failed to take anything more than a draw against Dunfermline on the penultimate day.

And so it was, on the final day of the season, Rangers were at Tannadice while the Hoops were entertaining St Johnstone at Celtic Park but entertainment is a word that can only be used with 20/20 hindsight as those 90 minutes were fraught with tension. Henrik Larsson and Harald Brattbakk scored the goals that stopped the 10 but seemingly everything won in the '90s came at a price as, just two days later, Jansen announced he was leaving.

WIM JANSEN HONOURS

League Championship (1)
1997/98

League Cup (1)
1997/98

SCOTTISH PREMIER DIVISION 1997/98

	PLD	W	D	L	F	A	PTS
CELTIC	36	22	8	6	64	24	74
Rangers	36	21	9	6	76	38	72
Hearts	36	19	10	7	70	46	67
Kilmarnock	36	13	11	12	40	52	50
St Johnstone	36	13	9	14	38	42	48
Aberdeen	36	9	12	15	39	53	39
Dundee Utd	36	8	13	15	43	51	37
Dunfermline	36	8	13	15	43	68	37
Motherwell	36	9	7	20	46	64	34
Hibernian	36	6	12	18	38	59	30

FORREST FIRE

INJURY may have deprived James Forrest from being on the pitch on the day the title was secured but his contribution to the triumph was invaluable. The 20-year-old has been a vital component of Neil Lennon's side throughout the entire campaign, starring in 41 games in all competitions until he was sidelined by a knock in the League Cup final.

One of Celtic's most potent attacking weapons, with his explosive pace, trickery and shooting ability, Forrest has also belied his tender years at times in the season by seizing responsibility on the pitch and dragging the team back into a game.

It was these types of displays which saw him recognised as one of FIFA's most exciting young players in world football in January.

A season of success both individually and collectively for the winger, he was delighted to round it off with his first League championship medal. He was a thoroughly deserving recipient.

"At the start of the season you aim to win the league and we have done that. It's the first time I have won it so obviously I'm buzzing," he said. "It's good for all the lads and hopefully we can get more under our belt now. We have won it once now and we want to kick on and try and win more.

"It's a great honour for me, and it just show where the team have come from last year – we have got better and better and hopefully we can keep doing that.

"It's good to have played so many games and I was gutted to be injured and miss the last few games. You want to be part of the big matches and I was disappointed to miss the Kilmarnock one but hopefully I can come back, fitter and better.

"It was class to be there and be a part of it. The boys put on an excellent performance. We have done that all season and we have deserved to win the league this year.

"The fans were excellent and they are why we do it every week and why we come into training," he added. "They give us the belief and it's good for us to repay them back by winning something."

Forrest lifted his first major honour last season when he helped the Hoops win the Scottish Cup. That was a memorable milestone in his career. However, he admitted that being crowned champions was something extra special.

"Obviously winning the league is different. It takes you the whole season to win it and it's a great feeling. All the boys have done well this season. We had a lot of injuries and we came through it.

"You're at a big club and people expect you to win things. That's what you want to do when you're here. You want to play in big games and hopefully I can win more trophies here."

At one point, Celtic trailed Rangers by 15 points but a 20-match run of successive domestic victories saw them storm to the league summit, a position they never looked in danger of surrendering.

Arguably, the catalyst for that shift in momentum was a game at, ironically, Rugby Park in October. At half-time, Celtic were trailing 3-0, their season in danger of going into freefall. However, helped through a tremendous performance by Forrest, the Hoops rallied in the second-half to secure a point.

"I think that was the turning point," he said. "If we had lost that it might have been different. But we came back and got a draw and I think that was vital.

"We always had belief and knew once that we had players to come back from injury. We also knew that Rangers would drop points and we would need to capitalise on that – I think we did that and showed good character.

"There's no argument about that. Throughout the season we have been the better team and hopefully we can still finish a good number of points above them."

"IT was a great performance, especially winning 6-0 here. I thought the lads were really good and we can celebrate the title now. We came here back in October and were 3-0 down at half-time. We went on and got the point that day and kicked on from there. To come from 15 points down and to go 11 points clear is really good-going.

"The team spirit is unbelievable and the coaches, everyone, has done their job and won the title here. Even though we lost to Kilmarnock in the League Cup final a few weeks ago we had to make it up to the fans and we did that by winning 6-0 and it was a brilliant performance.

"Charlie and Loovy scored great headers, and then Charlie did it with his right foot as well. But then he put another ball in for me to finish in the first-half and we kicked on then.

"The second-half wasn't as good as the first but we kept a clean sheet and Charlie did well to get Man of the Match. I got another one at the end and it was my first goal outside the box this season! There was probably a little slice on it but I'll take it."

- GARY HOOPER

"IT'S an unbelievable feeling to be a champion for Celtic. I think as a kid, supporting Celtic, I never thought I would be playing for them never mind winning the league with them. It's a dream come true and I'm delighted.

"I don't think anything has felt as good as this in my career so far. It's brilliant and it makes it even better after getting so close last year, it's even sweeter. It was great to cap off the day with a performance like that as well, the whole day was outstanding.

"People are going on like we were handed the title this year, but we were 15 points behind earlier in the season. It was an outstanding run we went on and to do a run like that anywhere in the world is unbelievable. The consistency we have shown this season has been outstanding so this title is thoroughly deserved.

"My personal opinion is that every team has a good run every season and then you hit a dip. Rangers started the season so well and we didn't so we knew we were going to get better and we thought it was only a matter of time until they hit a rocky patch. Their form dropped and that happens in football, while the only way we could have gone was up.

"This is a very young squad, definitely the youngest I've been involved with by a long way. That's great for the club because we all have our best years ahead of us so we can only improve and get better.

"I'm delighted for the gaffer as well, he's been outstanding. A lot of people would have chucked it in last year with everything that was going on but it just shows the sort of strong character he is - he's never going to walk away.

"Winning this drives us all on to win the Scottish Cup now. We were all disappointed losing the first cup final of the season but we're desperate to go on now and do the double."

- ANTHONY STOKES

FRASER'S GLOVE STORY

FRASER Forster believes the biggest factor behind Celtic's title triumph has been the unwavering self-belief among the players. Even at the bleakest point of the season, when the Hoops fell 15 points behind Rangers in November, the goalkeeper insists the entire dressing room remained convinced they could lift the championship.

That faith proved well-founded as Neil Lennon's men gradually gained forward momentum, before accelerating away from the rest of the pack following a remarkable 20-match winning run in domestic football.

Having being in such a difficult predicament a matter of months earlier, Celtic were crowned champions with five matches still to play thanks to the emphatic 6-0 rout of Kilmarnock. It was an incredible turnaround.

"The most important thing was probably just the belief," explained Forster. "We didn't start the season really well and it was just about maintaining that belief in ourselves, along with the belief the manager puts in you to still come back and win the league. I think it's that and just a great mental strength."

Although the Hoops had established a lead which was realistically unassailable to bridge, Forster admitted finally passing the finishing line, and doing so in such sparkling style, was a huge weight off the shoulders.

"I think everyone is just delighted by the way the season has gone," he said. "It's been a hard few weeks as we've been so far ahead. It's just been grinding out results and putting in that performance as well was brilliant."

The day the title was clinched will live long in the memory for Forster. Celtic supporters descended on Rugby Park, cramming into three of the four stands and creating an incredible party atmosphere.

It was matched by the display on the park which was simply scintillating as the Hoops demonstrated why they were worthy champions.

"You work hard all season and to become champions in the style we did as well was something special," said Forster. "It was absolutely brilliant. The fans were terrific. To sell out three-quarters of the stadium away from home would never really have happened anywhere else. It was a great day and it couldn't have gone any better than it did on the pitch.

"It was an unbelievable atmosphere for the full 90 minutes all the fans were singing. There was a real party atmosphere so it was just good that the lads could repay the fans and give them a performance like that.

"Obviously it was good after the game. I had won the league at Norwich but it's hard to compare the two really. There was a brilliant atmosphere after the game. You just work hard for so much of the season, so to win the league so comfortably in the end is absolutely brilliant."

Yet another clean sheet was recorded in the victory and a miserly rearguard has been one of the major reasons for the team's success this season, with Forster proving a reliable and assured last line of defence.

"Whichever back four has played has been terrific and all the lads have chipped in defensively and we have defended from the front as well," said Forster. "I have been delighted with how many clean sheets we have kept and we are only a few off from breaking last year's record. It would be nice to keep a few more and break that."

Although there is still an atmosphere of euphoria around the club, the management team and the players are already looking to build on the latest success. And with such a youthful squad, Forster is certain that the future is bright in Paradise.

"I think we have a very young squad and quite an experienced squad for everyone's age," he said. "Everyone has played a lot of games for how old they are. There is a terrific bunch of lads and everyone has really contributed so it's just a case of keeping the squad and moving forwards really. There is the chance of going to play in Europe as well, so it's all about taking that chance."

"IT feels so good to be a champion and I can't even describe how I'm feeling but I know it is a good feeling. It's the best feeling ever. It's a very special thing to win the league with a young team like this - that's not an easy thing to do. We are young but we have worked hard and we deserve to win the league.

"Missing games is not nice, I wanted to go out there and be a part of the team but I couldn't do it because I was suspended. It was a bit difficult for me but I have moved on now and I'm available again.

"I have learned not to do something so stupid again. It wasn't nice being suspended and it sets you back, but I was there to support the team and I just wanted to see them win. The players who were on the pitch did that and I was very happy for them.

"The fans have been with us through the good and tough times so we expected them to come out and support us again for this game - and they did, in a big number. I was very happy to see that.

"I didn't expect the fans to be back at the stadium waiting for us and cheering for us. It was a nice surprise. I am always surprised by the fans because they are so passionate. They are magnificent, not just at the games but outside as well. They came all the way back to the stadium after the game had finished, it was a very nice thing to see.

"They are like our family and we wanted to give them something back. We're very pleased for them. I have played for teams before with fans who love their club, but they are nowhere near as passionate as the Celtic supporters.

"The manager has been great for us and he has been working hard through difficult times. It hasn't been easy for him and I know he has been under a lot of pressure but he has handled everything well so I'm also pleased for him."

- VICTOR WANYAMA

"The 6-0 win over Kilmarnock was an incredible occasion. The first half was just sensational - the fans, the singing, the atmosphere. And the way we played, the tempo we played at, to come in at 4-0 was just a remarkable shift from the lads. So credit to everyone as we played very well.

"There are only a few occasions when I have taken note and forgotten about the game for a few milliseconds and just had a look around. There was one song when all the stands were singing to one another and the hairs on the back of my neck just stood up. I got goosebumps. It was just incredible.

"The only other time that's happened was when we played Rangers at home last season when the stadium did the Huddle when the score was at 3-0. That was amazing and was great to be part of.

"People who have been here a while like Browny and Charlie, the experienced lads who know what it's all about, they just take it with a pinch of salt. But for boys like me, Kelvin and Adam Matthews and the younger boys, it's an eye-opener to just how big this club is and if we can bring a good standard of European football next season, then that sort of support means anyone travelling to Celtic Park will be in fear of us."

- KRIS COMMONS

Martin O'Neill: 2000/01

IT'S fair to say that any new managerial appointment brings with it a certain air of expectancy but on June 1, 2000 the dreams went through the roof when Martin O'Neill stood on the steps of Celtic Park and announced: "I will do everything I possibly can to bring some success to this football club." Just 51 weeks and 48 domestic games later, the treble was glistening at Celtic Park for the first time since 1969 and for only the third time ever – some success?

Some tools of the trade were there when the Irishman arrived but he added to the kit-box and added in style with the likes of Chris Sutton, Alan Thompson and Neil Lennon making their way to Celtic Park as the new manager honed a team that would rewrite the history books.

If any further proof was needed that the Scottish football tide was making a dramatic turn, then it arrived on August 27, 2000 when Rangers turned up for the first big derby of the season. The piercing sunshine of this day couldn't have brightened Paradise up any more than the six goals, one as good as the next, that flew into the Ibrox team's net in what became known as the Demolition Derby – or simply the 6-2 game for those who prefer their red letter days described in more basic terms.

One swallow does not a summer make, though, and it was still early days in the championship race but the momentum rarely faltered and confidence increased when the League Cup was lifted on March 18 while results elsewhere ensured that the championship could be claimed on April 7 if the Celts won their three games that week.

Aberdeen and Dundee were taken care of before St Mirren turned up at a packed Celtic Park seemingly little more than lambs to the slaughter but at the end of the day it was a scuffed shot from Tommy Johnson that took the points and the title with another five games still to be played.

Dundee United and Hibernian as Scottish Cup opponents still stood in the way of the treble but the Tannadice side first, and then the Edinburgh club also fell to Celtic's superiority and the third piece of silverware was lifted on May 26.

MARTIN O'NEILL HONOURS

League Championships (3)
2000/01, 2001/02, 2003/04

Scottish Cups (3)
2001, 2004, 2005

League Cup (1)
2001

SCOTTISH PREMIER LEAGUE 2000/01

	PLD	W	D	L	F	A	PTS
CELTIC	38	31	4	3	90	29	97
Rangers	38	26	4	8	76	36	82
Hibernian	38	18	12	8	57	35	66
Kilmarnock	38	15	9	14	44	53	54
Hearts	38	14	10	14	56	50	52
Dundee	38	13	8	17	51	49	47
Aberdeen	38	11	12	15	45	52	45
Motherwell	38	12	7	19	42	56	43
Dunfermline	38	11	9	18	34	54	42
St Johnstone	38	9	13	16	40	56	40
Dundee Utd	38	9	8	21	38	63	35
St Mirren	38	8	6	24	32	72	30

Gordon Strachan: 2005/06

MORE than a few eyebrows were raised when Gordon Strachan was selected to replace the departing Martin O'Neill and they were followed by some smug 'I told you so' jibes when his first game turned out to be the disastrous European reverse to Artmedia Bratislava.

However, the critics were answered in the best possible way as Strachan joined that illustrious band of managers who lifted the title with Celtic at the very first time of asking. Indeed, despite a start which didn't exactly set the heather on fire – an opening-day 4-4 draw with Motherwell and a 3-1 defeat at Ibrox a few weeks later – Strachan's Celts sealed the league title in quick-fire style with six games still to be played.

The championship wasn't the only silverware claimed that season as a 3-0 win over Dunfermline on April 19 tied up the first trophy of the manager's reign when the League Cup was delivered to the boardroom thanks to goals from Maciej Zurawski, Shaun Maloney and Dion Dublin.

"Critics were answered in the best possible way as Strachan joined that illustrious band of managers who lifted the title with Celtic at the very first time of asking"

It was the holy grail of the championship that mattered most, though, and the Hoops went into that League Cup final on the back of a 13-game unbeaten run in the SPL as the challenge gained momentum with each passing game.

And, within 17 days of lifting the League Cup, the SPL trophy was added to the haul. Just three days after the final, Inverness CT were beaten 2-1 and the following weekend a 2-0 away win over Livingston meant the midweek visit of Hearts could be the title-clincher.

Big Bad John Hartson scored the only goal of the game on his 31st birthday and the flag fluttered over Paradise once more and, although Celtic drew three of their remaining six games, the Hoops won the title with 94 points while Hearts were in second place with 74 and Rangers lay in third with 73.

GORDON STRACHAN HONOURS

League Championships (3)
2005/06, 2006/07, 2007/08

Scottish Cups (1)
2007

League Cup (2)
2005/06, 2007/08

SCOTTISH PREMIER LEAGUE 2005/06

	PLD	W	D	L	F	A	PTS
CELTIC	38	28	7	3	93	37	91
Hearts	38	22	8	8	71	31	74
Rangers	38	21	10	7	67	37	73
Hibernian	38	17	5	16	61	56	56
Kilmarnock	38	15	10	13	63	64	55
Aberdeen	38	13	15	10	46	40	54
Inverness CT	38	15	13	10	51	38	58
Motherwell	38	13	10	15	55	61	49
Dundee Utd	38	7	12	19	41	66	33
Falkirk	38	8	9	21	35	64	33
Dunfermline	38	8	9	21	33	68	33
Livingston	38	4	6	28	25	79	18

next page: the players
who helped win the title

Clydesdale
Bank PREMIER
LEAGUE

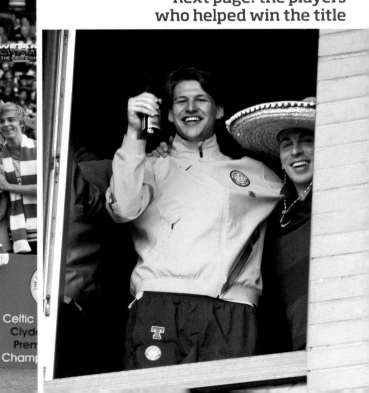

Scott BROWN

"We want to make Celtic Park a fortress this season so we have to start the way we mean to continue. It's always special playing at your own stadium and in front of your own support. It's great to see the crowd cheering and doing the Huddle, all that helps the players and it's fantastic to watch."

- SCOTT BROWN (August 2011)

SCOTT Brown has played a captain's role in driving Celtic towards the SPL title this season. The midfielder is one of the few players in the current squad who have won the championship before, having done so in 200/09, and his presence both on and off the park has been vital to the team's success.

The 26-year-old missed part of the season with an ankle injury picked up on international duty with Scotland, and after he limped off during the 4-2 defeat at Ibrox back in September, he was out of action until the end of November, when he returned for a Europa League clash with Atletico Madrid.

His return to the team also coincided with Celtic's remarkable run of victories which saw them overturn a 15-point deficit, and after a couple of substitute appearances at the beginning of December in the victories over Dundee United at Hearts, Brown has been a regular presence in Neil Lennon's starting XI.

The captain has also chipped in with a few goals as well, including a couple in the league. His first of the season came as the rain lashed St Mirren Park, and it was an exquisite left-foot finish from a short corner taken by Kris Commons. And Brown has also found himself on penalty duties for the team as well this season, though his spot-kick successes have so far all come in cup games. His other league goal was the opener in a 4-0 thrashing of Hearts at Tynecastle in early February.

Ask any of the Celtic team who the first name on the team-sheet should be and almost to a man they'll reply 'Scott Brown'. It is an indication of the value the player brings to the squad, and he is a thoroughly-deserving title-winning Celtic captain.

2011/12 STATS

17 Appearances

v Dundee United	(13/08/11)
v St Johnstone	(21/08/11)
v St Mirren	(28/08/11)
v Rangers	(18/09/11)
v St Johnstone	(18/12/11)
v Kilmarnock	(24/12/11)
v Rangers	(28/12/11)
v Dunfermline	(02/01/12)
v Dundee United	(14/01/12)
v St Mirren	(21/01/12)
v Hearts	(08/02/12)
v Inverness CT	(11/02/12)
v Hibernian	(19/02/12)
v Dunfermline	(27/02/12)
v Rangers	(25/03/12)
v St Johnstone	(01/04/12)
v Kilmarnock	(07/04/12)

2 Substitute

v Dundee United	(04/12/11)
v Hearts	(10/12/11)

2 Goals

v St Mirren	(21/01/12)
v Hearts	(08/02/12)

2 Yellow Cards

v Hearts	(08/02/12)
v Hibernian	(19/02/12)

stats correct as of April 7, 2012

"The first thing my father taught me when I came to European football in Germany 10 years ago was the importance of having good team-mates. This week I have finally realised what he meant. I was sent off in a vital match and all I could think about was that the defeat was all my fault. Then what my father told me all those years ago became true. Everyone came up to me and put their arm round my shoulder and told me I didn't deserve to be sent off."

- CHA (March 2012)

Cha DU-RI

CELTIC'S South Korean defender has been involved in a three-way battle for the right-back slot with Mark Wilson and Adam Matthews, who joined the club last summer from Cardiff City. And that competition became even more ferocious following the arrival of Swedish internationalist, Mikael Lustig, during the January transfer window.

Cha Du-Ri is an experienced defender who joined Celtic from German club, Freiburg in 2010. He comes from good footballing stock, with his father, Cha Bum-Kun having also been a professional footballer in Germany, and an internationalist with South Korea.

In Cha's first season at Celtic, he made 20 appearances for the first-team, memorably scoring one goal in the 2-0 Boxing Day victory over St Johnstone at Celtic Park, but the rest of the campaign was unfortunately curtailed by injury. This season, he's played 13 times, including 10

starts, with Adam Matthews proving a tough rival to replace at right-back.

Most recently, the South Korean internationalist was in the starting XI for the match at the end of March against Rangers, with Matthews switching to the left-back role. Unfortunately, that was a game which Cha won't want to remember as he was red-carded just before the half-hour mark after a challenge with Lee Wallace. It was a harsh red card, and one that left the Celtic players, management and fans bemused. The club immediately appealed against the red card.

The dismissal was a blow to the team as well as to the player, which meant he would automatically miss the next game as the Hoops closed in on the title. Cha's presence in the squad has also helped in the development of his fellow countryman, Ki Sung Yueng, who at just 23, has looked to the older player for help and guidance in living and playing in another country.

2011/12 STATS

10 Appearances

v St Mirren	(28/08/11)
v Kilmarnock	(15/10/11)
v Motherwell	(06/11/11)
v Dundee United	(04/12/11)
v Hearts	(10/12/11)
v St Johnstone	(18/12/11)
v Kilmarnock	(24/12/11)
v St Mirren	(21/01/12)
v Dunfermline	(27/02/12)
v Rangers	(25/03/12)

3 Substitute

v Dunfermline	(02/01/12)
v Motherwell	(25/02/12)
v Aberdeen	(03/03/12)

1 Yellow Card

v St Mirren	(21/01/12)

1 Red Card

v Rangers	(25/03/12)

stats correct as of April 7, 2012

Kris COMMONS

TO say that Kris Commons has endured a frustrating season would be an understatement. The player had joined the club last January from Derby County, and his impact was immediate, with a wonderful goal at Hampden in the semi-final of the League Cup against Aberdeen. He would go on to score a total of 15 goals, becoming a vital player.

Season 2011/12, however, has not brought the same return from the player, who has found his campaign disrupted by a series of troublesome injuries, preventing him from getting a consistent run in the team. Remarkably, Commons has also still to find the net this season.

One statistic he won't want to be reminded of is the red card he picked up at Tynecastle back in October. It had been his first start in almost two months, but he picked up a straight red for a challenge on Adrian Mrowiec. At that point the Hoops were trailing by a goal, and they would go on to lose the match 2-0.

Commons remains a vital member of the squad, however, and his introduction from the substitutes' bench can often help turn a game or further strengthen Celtic's grip on proceedings. The 2-0 victory over St Mirren in January this year was a perfect example of that, with his intelligence on the ball a vital ingredient in Neil Lennon's side eventually winning the match.

And he has come back to full fitness at a vital time of the campaign for the Hoops, giving the manager another strong attacking option to his squad.

"Being in the tunnel, and then the handshakes isn't too bad, but when we do the Huddle and you hear the roar it gives you goose-bumps on the back of your neck. You just want to get on with it, do your best and score some goals."

- KRIS COMMONS (February 2012)

2011/12 STATS

11 Appearances

v Hibernian	(24/07/11)
v Aberdeen	(07/08/11)
v Dundee United	(13/08/11)
v St Johnstone	(21/08/11)
v Hearts	(02/10/11)
v Motherwell	(06/11/11)
v Dunfermline	(23/11/11)
v Dunfermline	(22/02/12)
v Aberdeen	(03/03/12)
v St Johnstone	(01/04/12)
v Kilmarnock	(07/04/12)

7 Substitute

v Motherwell	(10/09/11)
v Inverness CT	(19/11/11)
v St Mirren	(21/01/12)
v Inverness CT	(11/02/12)
v Hibernian	(19/02/12)
v Motherwell	(25/02/12)
v Rangers	(25/03/12)

1 Red Card

v Hearts	(02/10/11)

stats correct as of April 7, 2012

James FORREST

"I was sitting in with the Celtic fans at Ibrox and they were class. I was with a few of the boys who weren't in the squad, the fans spotted us and they were good with us. It's been a good while since I sat in the stand with them and I know it means a lot to the fans but I'd still rather I was out playing on the pitch."

- JAMES FORREST (March 2012)

A CANDIDATE for both the Player and Young Player of the Year Awards this season, James Forrest has been one of Celtic's most outstanding performers throughout the campaign. The 20-year-old is only in his second full season as a first-team player but he is already an integral part of Neil Lennon's squad, and his appearance record shows that, when fit, he generally plays.

He's also heading towards double figures in league goals this season, having opened his account back in August in the first home SPL game of the campaign, netting in the 5-1 victory over Dundee United. He followed that up just a couple of weeks later with a double in the 4-0 win against Motherwell. And one of his most important goals came in the 2-0 win away to St Mirren in January, breaking the deadlock in a tight game.

If Forrest has been an important scorer and provider of goals this season, then perhaps his stand-out performance came in the 3-3 draw against Kilmarnock at Rugby Park. With Celtic trailing 3-0 at half-time, it was the young Celt who seemed to drive the team forward and drag them back into the match with an impressive display of skill, determination and an incredible desire not to accept defeat.

The only real disappointment for Forrest this season was the injury he picked up late in the League Cup final defeat to Kilmarnock, which ruled him out of the league game at Ibrox the following weekend.

He has also pushed himself into the international set-up, and the graduate of the Celtic Youth Academy is certainly a player who excites supporters, inspires the younger players coming through the ranks at the club and thoroughly deserves any praise or accolades which come his way for his contribution this season.

2011/12 STATS

23 Appearances

v St Mirren	(28/08/11)
v Motherwell	(10/09/11)
v Inverness CT	(24/09/11)
v Hearts	(02/10/11)
v Kilmarnock	(15/10/11)
v Aberdeen	(23/10/11)
v Hibernian	(29/10/11)
v Motherwell	(06/11/11)
v Inverness CT	(19/11/11)
v Dunfermline	(23/11/11)
v St Mirren	(26/11/11)
v Dundee United	(04/12/11)
v Hearts	(10/12/11)
v St Johnstone	(18/12/11)
v Kilmarnock	(24/12/11)
v Rangers	(28/12/11)
v Dunfermline	(02/01/12)
v St Mirren	(21/01/12)
v Hearts	(08/02/12)
v Inverness CT	(11/02/12)
v Hibernian	(19/02/12)
v Motherwell	(25/02/12)
v Aberdeen	(03/03/12)

6 Substitute

v Hibernian	(24/07/11)
v Aberdeen	(07/08/11)
v Dundee United	(13/08/11)
v St Johnstone	(21/08/11)
v Rangers	(18/09/11)
v Dunfermline	(22/02/12)

7 Goals

v Dundee United	(13/08/11)
v Motherwell	(10/09/11)
v Motherwell	(10/09/11)
v Inverness CT	(24/09/11)
v Dunfermline	(23/11/11)
v St Mirren	(21/01/12)
v Dunfermline	(22/02/12)

1 Yellow Card

v Kilmarnock	(15/10/11)

stats correct as of April 7, 2012

Fraser FORSTER

"That was my first penalty save up here and I suppose it was overdue, but I didn't expect it to feel this good. I thought it was a soft penalty but it didn't matter in the end. I didn't know what way he was going to send the ball but I had a feeling in his run-up and guessed right. The save was massive but time seemed to drag after it and it felt like the clock wasn't moving."

- FRASER FORSTER (December 2011)

CELTIC'S first-choice goalkeeper has been the model of consistency since returning to the club for a second loan period. He missed the first three league games of the campaign, during which time Lukasz Zaluska proved a more than able deputy, but the big Englishman, standing tall at 6ft 7", has been the man in possession of the No.1 jersey throughout the season.

With 17 clean sheets so far this season, he has been in impressive form and that has provided the foundation for Celtic's success. It can be a lonely job being the Celtic goalkeeper, with the team usually enjoying the lion's share of possession and the play generally in the opposition half of the field. However, it means that the man between the sticks needs to remain concentrated so that, when he is called into action, he can prevent the opposition from scoring.

Forster has been superb in this regard, and he has produced vital saves in a number of games which have helped the team on to eventual victory. He is also a near ever-present, having only missed those opening three SPL games because he had not yet rejoined the club.

The one Fraser Forster moment which stands out for most supporters this season has to be his penalty save against Hearts at Celtic Park back in December last year. It was also a pivotal moment in the campaign. The Hoops had got back to winning ways, with four victories in a row when they faced Hearts. And Victor Wanyama appeared to have sealed all three points with his first goal for the club. However, a last-minute penalty for the visitors threatened to derail Celtic's run until Forster stepped forward and saved Eggert Jonsson's penalty. It was a vital save, a vital victory and a sign, if any was needed, of Forster's quality between the sticks.

2011/12 STATS

30 Appearances

v St Johnstone	(21/08/11)
v St Mirren	(28/08/11)
v Motherwell	(10/09/11)
v Rangers	(18/09/11)
v Inverness CT	(24/09/11)
v Hearts	(02/10/11)
v Kilmarnock	(15/10/11)
v Aberdeen	(23/10/11)
v Hibernian	(29/10/11)
v Motherwell	(06/11/11)
v Inverness CT	(19/11/11)
v Dunfermline	(23/11/11)
v St Mirren	(26/11/11)
v Dundee United	(04/12/11)
v Hearts	(10/12/11)
v St Johnstone	(18/12/11)
v Kilmarnock	(24/12/11)
v Rangers	(28/12/11)
v Dunfermline	(02/01/12)
v Dundee United	(14/01/12)
v St Mirren	(21/01/12)
v Hearts	(08/02/12)
v Inverness CT	(11/02/12)
v Hibernian	(19/02/12)
v Dunfermline	(22/02/12)
v Motherwell	(25/02/12)
v Aberdeen	(03/03/12)
v Rangers	(25/03/12)
v St Johnstone	(01/04/12)
v Kilmarnock	(07/04/12)

1 Yellow Card

v Dunfermline	(23/11/11)

stats correct as of April 7, 2012

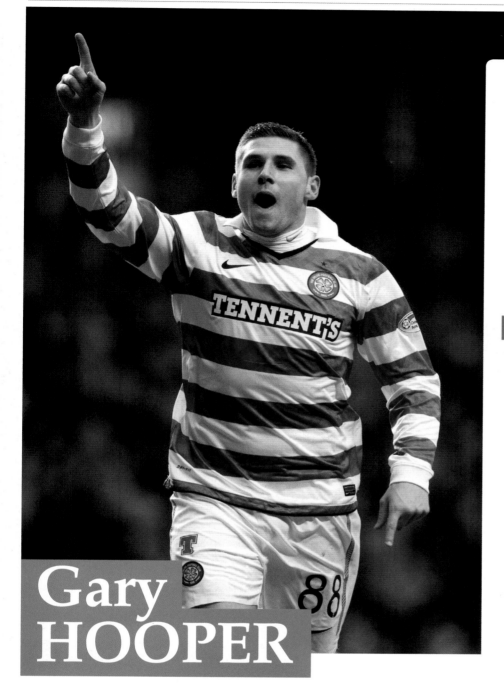

Gary HOOPER

"I think I've improved recently overall - I have maybe got fitter and stronger. Last season the team performed on and off, and I was probably the same, but we've all improved a lot this year."

- GARY HOOPER (February 2012)

2011/12 STATS

30 Appearances

v Hibernian	(24/07/11)
v Aberdeen	(07/08/11)
v Dundee United	(13/08/11)
v St Mirren	(28/08/11)
v Motherwell	(10/09/11)
v Rangers	(18/09/11)
v Inverness CT	(24/09/11)
v Hearts	(02/10/11)
v Kilmarnock	(15/10/11)
v Aberdeen	(23/10/11)
v Hibernian	(29/10/11)
v Inverness CT	(19/11/11)
v Dunfermline	(23/11/11)
v St Mirren	(26/11/11)
v Dundee United	(04/12/11)
v Hearts	(10/12/11)
v St Johnstone	(18/12/11)
v Kilmarnock	(24/12/11)
v Rangers	(28/12/11)
v Dunfermline	(02/01/12)
v Dundee United	(14/01/12)
v St Mirren	(21/01/12)
v Hearts	(08/02/12)
v Inverness CT	(11/02/12)
v Hibernian	(19/02/12)
v Dunfermline	(22/02/12)
v Motherwell	(25/02/12)
v Aberdeen	(03/03/12)
v St Johnstone	(01/04/12)
v Kilmarnock	(07/04/12)

1 Substitute

v Motherwell	(06/11/11)

18 Goals

v Dundee United	(13/08/11)
v St Mirren	(28/08/11)
v St Mirren	(28/08/11)
v Rangers	(18/09/11)
v Motherwell	(06/11/11)
v Dunfermline	(23/11/11)
v St Mirren	(26/11/11)
v St Mirren	(26/11/11)
v St Mirren	(26/11/11)
v Dundee United	(04/12/11)
v St Johnstone	(18/12/11)
v Dundee United	(14/01/12)
v Hearts	(08/02/12)
v Hibernian	(19/02/12)
v Hibernian	(19/02/12)
v Motherwell	(25/02/12)
v Kilmarnock	(07/04/12)
v Kilmarnock	(07/04/12)

1 Yellow Card

v Motherwell	(10/09/11)

stats correct as of April 7, 2012

FOR the second season in a row, Gary Hooper is battling it out with Anthony Stokes for the title of Celtic's top goalscorer. The Englishman has enjoyed another impressive season in the Hoops, and is a vital player for the team. You only have to look at his appearances to realise that, when he's fit, Gary Hooper generally starts for Celtic.

So it was a blow to Neil Lennon when Hooper picked up an injury in the League Cup final and was only able to make it on to the bench for the subsequent SPL game at Ibrox. It was in the earlier derby match at the same ground that Hooper scored one of his best goals of the season. It was a great through ball from Scott Brown to the striker, who controlled it and fired a low, right-foot shot beyond Allan McGregor and into the net.

Hooper's eye for goal is instinctive and unerring, and he has chipped in with a variety of goals, some of them spectacular, and some tap-ins from inside the six-yard box. He knows where he should be in the penalty area and he knows how to finish. And whether leading the line on his own or playing alongside Anthony Stokes or Georgios Samaras, the Englishman is always a goal threat.

Indeed, there was some surprise that Hooper's form, not just this season but since he has arrived at Celtic, has not yet been rewarded with a call-up to the England squad. The English national side does not have an abundance of strikers to call upon, and Hooper certainly merits his chance.

In the meantime, he remains a vital part of Neil Lennon's squad, and his goals are one of the main reasons that Celtic are SPL champions for 2011/12.

> *"I'm so happy to sign a new deal with Celtic and want to be a success here and prove to everyone what I can do for this club, and to have success in the league, in the cups and in Europe. All my focus is just on football now."*
>
> — *BERAM KAYAL (October 2011)*

Beram KAYAL

IT was a bad tackle from Lee McCulloch which effectively ended Beram Kayal's season. The influential midfielder had been in outstanding form as Celtic put together a string of results that would wipe out a 15-point deficit and see them return to the top of the table with a 1-0 win over Rangers in the last game of 2011.

Kayal, however, wasn't able to enjoy the celebrations at the end of the game, having been forced out of the game on 77 minutes. And subsequent scans revealed ankle ligament damage that ruled him out of action for a few months. Celtic's midfield is a strong area of the team, with competition for places fierce, but Kayal was certainly one of the first names on the team-sheet when he was fit, and it is to the credit of the rest of the squad that they did adapt to cope with the loss of such an important player.

The Israeli internationalist quickly became a fans' favourite since arriving at the club from Maccabi

Haifa in 2010. He hadn't managed to get on the score-sheet in 2011/12 before picking up the serious injury, but his presence in the heart of the Celtic midfield was invaluable. He had managed 18 appearances up until that point, and the fact they were all starts is an indication of his importance within Neil Lennon's squad.

Kayal deserves great credit for his contribution to the title-winning success, and it's hoped he will return, fully fit, for the new campaign as the Hoops aim to make it two-in-a-row.

2011/12 STATS

18 Appearances

v Hibernian	(24/07/11)
v Aberdeen	(07/08/11)
v St Mirren	(28/08/11)
v Motherwell	(10/09/11)
v Rangers	(18/09/11)
v Inverness CT	(24/09/11)
v Kilmarnock	(15/10/11)
v Aberdeen	(23/10/11)
v Hibernian	(29/10/11)
v Motherwell	(06/11/11)
v Inverness CT	(19/11/11)
v Dunfermline	(23/11/11)
v St Mirren	(26/11/11)
v Dundee United	(04/12/11)
v Hearts	(10/12/11)
v St Johnstone	(18/12/11)
v Kilmarnock	(24/12/11)
v Rangers	(28/12/11)

4 Yellow Cards

v Kilmarnock	(15/10/11)
v Inverness CT	(19/11/11)
v St Johnstone	(18/12/11)
v Kilmarnock	(24/12/11）

stats correct as of April 7, 2012

Ki
SUNG-YUENG

> *"The Cha has power and speed and has shown that he is one of the best full backs in the country. He and James Forrest have great pace down that side. I've been very impressed with him and pleased to play alongside him as well."*
>
> — *KI SUNG YUENG* (December 2011)

2011/12 STATS

20 Appearances

v Hibernian	(24/07/11)
v Aberdeen	(07/08/11)
v Dundee United	(13/08/11)
v St Johnstone	(21/08/11)
v St Mirren	(28/08/11)
v Motherwell	(10/09/11)
v Rangers	(18/09/11)
v Inverness CT	(24/09/11)
v Hearts	(02/10/11)
v Kilmarnock	(15/10/11)
v Aberdeen	(23/10/11)
v Hibernian	(29/10/11)
v St Johnstone	(18/12/11)
v Kilmarnock	(24/12/11)
v St Mirren	(21/01/12)
v Dunfermline	(22/02/12)
v Motherwell	(25/02/12)
v Aberdeen	(03/03/12)
v Rangers	(25/03/12)
v Kilmarnock	(07/04/12)

9 Substitute

v Inverness CT	(19/11/11)
v Dundee United	(04/12/11)
v Hearts	(10/12/11)
v Rangers	(28/12/11)
v Dunfermline	(02/01/12)
v Dundee United	(14/01/12)
v Inverness CT	(11/02/12)
v Hibernian	(19/02/12)
v St Johnstone	(01/04/12)

6 Goals

v Hibernian	(24/07/11)
v Dundee United	(13/08/11)
v Motherwell	(10/09/11)
v Aberdeen	(23/10/11)
v St Johnstone	(18/12/11)
v Hibernian	(19/02/12)

3 Yellow Cards

v Dundee United	(13/08/11)
v Hearts	(02/10/11)
v Dunfermline	(02/01/12)

stats correct as of April 7, 2012

KI Sung Yueng had signed off last season with a spectacular goal in the Scottish Cup final victory over Motherwell, and he began the new campaign in similar fashion, scoring with another thunderous shot on the opening day of the season as Celtic beat Hibernian 2-0 at Easter Road.

The Korean midfielder followed that home with another goal in the first home league match of the campaign, in a 5-1 victory over Dundee United, and he's managed to score six SPL goals so far in 2011/12. This tally includes the rather fortuitous one he netted in the 5-0 win over Hibernian at Easter Road in February. Kris Commons' shot was wildly off target but landed perfectly in the path of Ki, who had surged into the penalty area, and he instinctively steered the ball into the Hibs net.

Ki is still only 23 but already he has a wealth of experience at club and international level. An important figure in the South Korea national side, during the course of the season, he has had to contend with a heavy travelling schedule whenever there have been games for his country and, indeed, he missed the 1-1 draw with Aberdeen in March because he didn't return on time from a midweek match with South Korea.

He is a composed player in the middle of the park, able to put his foot on the ball and dictate the pace of the game, and he has been an important part of Celtic's success this season. He has also benefited from having fellow countryman, Cha Di-Ri, in the Celtic squad as well.

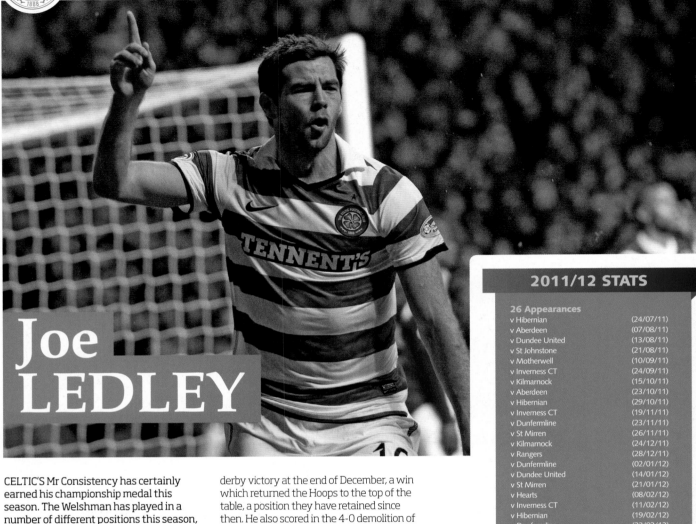

Joe LEDLEY

CELTIC'S Mr Consistency has certainly earned his championship medal this season. The Welshman has played in a number of different positions this season, often covering at left back, and he has never let the team down. It's fair to assume that, when he's fit, Joe Ledley is one of the first names on Neil Lennon's team-sheet.

While he admits he prefers playing midfield, and he's played either in the centre of the park or wide left, Ledley simply plays where he is asked to, always without fuss or complaint, and it's this attitude, allied to his ability, which has made him such a key figure for Celtic, and such a favourite with the fans.

His work-rate is impressive – he never seems to stop running – and he has also managed to pop up with some vital goals during the campaign, including the winning goal in the derby victory at the end of December, a win which returned the Hoops to the top of the table, a position they have retained since then. He also scored in the 4-0 demolition of Hearts at Tynecastle in February.

There is no doubt that Ledley has been a superb acquisition by Neil Lennon for Celtic, and the Welsh internationalist certainly enjoys playing for the Hoops. Last season, Ledley suffered a hamstring injury which ruled him out of the vital run-in to the term, but this time around he has been able to savour a title triumph with Celtic, and a thoroughly deserved one at that.

He has missed very few games for the Hoops this season and is one of the players in the running for the Celtic Player of the Year Award, voted for by the fans, and while he has a number of rivals, he would certainly be a popular and worthy winner.

2011/12 STATS

26 Appearances

v Hibernian	(24/07/11)
v Aberdeen	(07/08/11)
v Dundee United	(13/08/11)
v St Johnstone	(21/08/11)
v Motherwell	(10/09/11)
v Inverness CT	(24/09/11)
v Kilmarnock	(15/10/11)
v Aberdeen	(23/10/11)
v Hibernian	(29/10/11)
v Inverness CT	(19/11/11)
v Dunfermline	(23/11/11)
v St Mirren	(26/11/11)
v Kilmarnock	(24/12/11)
v Rangers	(28/12/11)
v Dunfermline	(02/01/12)
v Dundee United	(14/01/12)
v St Mirren	(21/01/12)
v Hearts	(08/02/12)
v Inverness CT	(11/02/12)
v Hibernian	(19/02/12)
v Dunfermline	(22/02/12)
v Motherwell	(25/02/12)
v Aberdeen	(03/03/12)
v Rangers	(25/03/12)
v St Johnstone	(01/04/12)
v Kilmarnock	(07/04/12)

1 Substitute

v St Mirren	(28/08/11)

1 Yellow Card

v Kilmarnock	(07/04/12)

7 Goals

v Dundee United	(13/08/11)
v Motherwell	(10/09/11)
v Inverness CT	(24/09/11)
v Rangers	(28/12/11)
v Hearts	(08/02/12)
v Inverness CT	(11/02/12)
v Kilmarnock	(07/04/12)

stats correct as of April 7, 2012

"The fans give us all a massive boost and a buzz when you go into the games and you just want to try and work as hard as you can for them and try and get the win for them, as they had obviously spent a lot of money for tickets and things like that. We just want to try and go out there in games and get the win for them and for ourselves."

- JOE LEDLEY *(March 2012)*

"When you're out for that long, and the team perform as well as they did, it's always going to be difficult to change the team. The players played really well, Thomas and Kelvin have been doing well and Charlie has been unbelievable for the whole season."

- DANIEL MAJSTOROVIC
(February 2012)

Daniel
MAJSTOROVIC

DANIEL Majstorovic can lay claim to being the unluckiest player at Celtic Park this season, having suffered two serious injuries during the campaign. The first came back in December, when he fractured his cheekbone following an accidental clash with a St Johnstone player.

The injury meant an enforced period on the sidelines but he returned at the beginning of February determined to force his way back into the team and play his part in the title run-in. But while on international duty with Sweden at the end of February, he ruptured the cruciate ligament in his left knee, ruling him out for the rest of the season.

To compound the misery for the defender, the injury means he will also miss Sweden's participation in this summer's European Championships, something he had been looking forward to, since it was his first opportunity to play at a major finals tournament.

Majstorovic's last action for Celtic this season was to get red-carded during the home game against Inverness Caley Thistle in February. It appeared a harsh decision at the time, with the defender penalised for what was deemed a last-man challenge, and after Celtic lodged an appeal, the red card was rescinded. However, Majstorovic subsequently suffered his injury, meaning he has missed the run to the title.

2011/12 STATS

15 Appearances

v Aberdeen	(07/08/11)
v Dundee United	(13/08/11)
v St Johnstone	(21/08/11)
v St Mirren	(28/08/11)
v Inverness CT	(24/09/11)
v Hearts	(02/10/11)
v Kilmarnock	(15/10/11)
v Motherwell	(06/11/11)
v Inverness CT	(19/11/11)
v Dunfermline	(23/11/11)
v St Mirren	(26/11/11)
v Dundee United	(04/12/11)
v Hearts	(10/12/11)
v St Johnstone	(18/12/11)
v Inverness CT	(11/02/12)

2 Substitute

v Aberdeen	(23/10/11)
v Hearts	(08/02/12)

2 Yellow Cards

v Aberdeen	(07/08/11)
v Inverness CT	(19/11/11)

1 Red Card

v Inverness CT	(11/02/12)
(Red card later rescinded)	

stats correct as of April 7, 2012

"If we keep this bunch of players around for a long time we can do something special at Celtic. The average age is about 24, which is really young in football terms for a top team, so we can only get better with experience and I think that's what we will do."

- *ADAM MATTHEWS* (April 2012)

Adam
MATTHEWS

SOMETIMES you have to remind yourself that Adam Matthews is only 20-years-old, such has been the consistency and maturity shown by the player throughout the season. Indeed, he joined the club from Cardiff City as a teenager, and while many observers would have presumed he'd have played a supporting role this season, it has been anything but.

Matthews, who is also now a full Welsh internationalist, has established himself as a first-team regular and the top choice at right-back, which is a fiercely competitive position, with Cha Du-Ri, Mark Wilson and, now, Mikael Lustig, all trying to lay claim to that berth in the team.

He made his league debut at the beginning of August in the victory over Aberdeen, and since then he has never looked back. He has also been called upon to slot into the left-back

position on occasion as well, and he has done so with relative ease.

The only thing missing from a perfect debut season for Matthews would be a Celtic goal, with the young Welshman still waiting to hit the back of the net for the Hoops. He has shown an impressive degree of consistency, and he has managed to avoid picking up any cautions in the SPL. His only yellow card of the campaign came in the League Cup victory over Ross County.

It has also helped Matthews to settle into his new surroundings by having fellow countryman, Joe Ledley, already at Celtic. The two players were team-mates at Cardiff, and have now linked up in Glasgow, with Neil Lennon's side benefiting. Matthews can only continue to improve, which will be great news for the Hoops fans, and he is another candidate for Player of the Year.

2011/12 STATS

22 Appearances

v Aberdeen	(07/08/11)
v St Johnstone	(21/08/11)
v Motherwell	(10/09/11)
v Inverness CT	(24/09/11)
v Hearts	(02/10/11)
v Kilmarnock	(15/10/11)
v Aberdeen	(23/10/11)
v Hibernian	(29/10/11)
v Motherwell	(06/11/11)
v Inverness CT	(19/11/11)
v Dunfermline	(23/11/11)
v St Mirren	(26/11/11)
v Dundee United	(04/12/11)
v Rangers	(28/12/11)
v Dunfermline	(02/01/12)
v Dundee United	(14/01/12)
v Hearts	(08/02/12)
v Inverness CT	(11/02/12)
v Hibernian	(19/02/12)
v Motherwell	(25/02/12)
v Rangers	(25/03/12)
v Kilmarnock	(07/04/12)

2 Substitute

v St Mirren	(21/01/12)
v St Johnstone	(01/04/12)

stats correct as of April 7, 2012

Charlie MULGREW

2011/12 STATS

25 Appearances

v Dundee United	(13/08/11)
v St Johnstone	(21/08/11)
v St Mirren	(28/08/11)
v Motherwell	(10/09/11)
v Rangers	(18/09/11)
v Hearts	(02/10/11)
v Kilmarnock	(15/10/11)
v Aberdeen	(23/10/11)
v Hibernian	(29/10/11)
v Hearts	(10/12/11)
v St Johnstone	(18/12/11)
v Kilmarnock	(24/12/11)
v Rangers	(28/12/11)
v Dunfermline	(02/01/12)
v Dundee United	(14/01/12)
v St Mirren	(21/01/12)
v Hearts	(08/02/12)
v Inverness CT	(11/02/12)
v Hibernian	(19/02/12)
v Dunfermline	(22/02/12)
v Motherwell	(25/02/12)
v Aberdeen	(03/03/12)
v Rangers	(25/03/12)
v St Johnstone	(01/04/12)
v Kilmarnock	(07/04/12)

1 Substitute

v Aberdeen	(07/08/11)

7 Goals

v Kilmarnock	(15/10/11)
v Aberdeen	(23/10/11)
v Dunfermline	(02/01/12)
v Hibernian	(19/02/12)
v Dunfermline	(22/02/12)
v Kilmarnock	(07/04/12)
v Kilmarnock	(07/04/12)

2 Yellow Cards

v Aberdeen	(23/10/11)
v Hearts	(08/02/12)

1 Red Card

v Rangers	(18/11/11)

stats correct as of April 7, 2012

"The manager has a good attitude and it's a good bunch of lads – we're all working towards the same goal. There are a lot of us around the same age, and that probably helps us. We're heading for the peak of our football careers together so it's all good at the moment."

- CHARLIE MULGREW (February 2012)

CHARLIE Mulgrew has been an outstanding performer for Celtic throughout the season and has been a real driving force in the Hoops' march to the SPL title. His performances have also earned him his first full international cap for Scotland, and it's no more than the defender deserves.

Mulgrew is another player who has played in a number of different positions this season, and whether at centre-half, left-back, left midfield or even in the centre of midfield, he has been a model of reliability. Not only that, but his ability from set-pieces is a potent weapon in Celtic's armoury.

He has scored five league goals, and set up many more, though it was his equalising goal in the 3-3 draw with Kilmarncok at Rugby Park last October which remains a pivotal moment in the season. It rescued the unlikeliest of draws for Neil Lennon's side, who had trailed 3-0 at half-time, and it also kick-started the remarkable turnaround in fortunes which saw the Hoops overturn a 15-point deficit to win the title.

Mulgrew is enjoying his second spell with the club, having come through the ranks of the Youth Academy before leaving for Wolves and then Aberdeen, and he has worked hard to establish himself in the side since returning to Celtic Park. He is also a Celtic fan and knows just how much it means to his fellow supporters to bring the title back to Paradise.

And Mulgrew will certainly be in the running for the Celtic Player of the Year Award, as well as the other honours voted for by his fellow players and also the Scottish football writers. If he should pick up any, or all of those awards, there are very few who would complain that he doesn't deserve it.

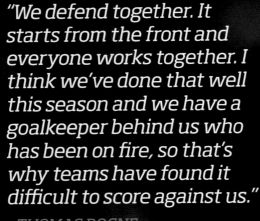

"We defend together. It starts from the front and everyone works together. I think we've done that well this season and we have a goalkeeper behind us who has been on fire, so that's why teams have found it difficult to score against us."

– THOMAS ROGNE (March 2012)

Thomas ROGNE

THOMAS Rogne is another young player who has made an important contribution to Celtic's title-winning campaign, though he has had to bide his time to get into the starting XI. An injury picked up during the pre-season tour of Australia was a setback for Rogne, and it's really been since the turn of the year that has pushed himself into the side.

He was in the team that beat Rangers 1-0 at the end of December to go back to the top of the SPL table, and he produced an outstanding performance that night, coping with the physical challenges of a Glasgow derby, and when fit, he's been in the team since then. He also scored his only goal of the season against Rangers, though it was in the 3-2 defeat at Ibrox in March.

Rogne can be a stylish defender when he wants

to be, but he's also tough and uncompromising and a very difficult player for any opposition forward. And his performances for Celtic this season also saw him rewarded with his first full international cap for Norway.

With Daniel Majstorovic out for the season with a ruptured cruciate ligament, it has been fortuitous that Rogne is now restored to full fitness and able to take his place in the heart of the Celtic defence, either alongside Kelvin Wilson, Charlie Mulgrew, or even Victor Wanyama on occasion.

And it augurs well for Celtic's future that Rogne, at only 21, is another young player with the potential to be at the club for many seasons to come, helping to deliver more success to Paradise.

2011/12 STATS

12 Appearances

v Hibernian	(29/10/11)
v Motherwell	(06/11/11)
v Rangers	(28/12/11)
v Dunfermline	(02/01/12)
v Dundee United	(14/01/12)
v St Mirren	(21/01/12)
v Hearts	(08/02/12)
v Hibernian	(19/02/12)
v Motherwell	(25/02/12)
v Aberdeen	(03/03/12)
v Rangers	(25/03/12)
v St Johnstone	(01/04/12)

2 Substitute

v St Johnstone	(18/12/11)
v Kilmarnock	(24/12/11)

1 Goal

v Rangers	(25/03/12)

2 Yellow Cards

v St Mirren	(21/01/12)
v Aberdeen	(03/03/12)

stats correct as of April 7, 2012

Georgios SAMARAS

THE Celtic management team have always been aware of Georgios Samaras' outstanding ability. They just wanted him to show it on a more consistent basis. And the Greek forward has certainly obliged this season, with his contribution one of the main factors in Celtic's incredible run of 20 consecutive domestic wins in all competitions.

The run propelled Celtic into pole position in the league, and ensured that the SPL title has returned to Paradise. And Samaras has been instrumental in all of that. At times, the word 'unplayable' has been used in a complimentary sense to describe the 27-year-old, and when he's in full flow, defences have found it difficult to cope with him.

He has been deployed either on the left of a four or five-man midfield, or straight through the middle as a lone striker or alongside Anthony Stokes or Gary Hooper. Wherever he has been asked to play, his contribution has been superb, and he has laid on a number of goals along the way. He's also scored a few as well, including one in the 2-0 victory over St Johnstone which put Celtic within a point of securing the title.

Samaras is focused on delivering silverware to Celtic, but he is also looking forward to the European Championships to be held in Poland and Ukraine this summer. Greece, who won the competition in 2004, are competing in the finals, and the Celtic striker is a mainstay of the squad.

He is one of the most experienced players in the Celtic squad, and is also one of the few who has won the title before with the Hoops, back in 2008 as a loan Celt and again in 2009 after making his move to Paradise a permanent one, and he has now made it three title wins as a Celtic player.

"We're going to win the title as a team – not as individuals and that's what it's all about. If somebody wants to win things as an individual they can play golf or tennis and be happy with that, but I'm in a team."

- GEORGIOS SAMARAS (April 2012)

2011/12 STATS

18 appearances

v Rangers	(18/09/11)
v Motherwell	(06/11/11)
v Inverness CT	(19/11/11)
v St Mirren	(26/11/11)
v Dundee United	(04/12/11)
v Hearts	(10/12/11)
v St Johnstone	(18/12/11)
v Kilmarnock	(24/12/11)
v Rangers	(28/12/11)
v Dunfermline	(02/01/12)
v Dundee United	(14/01/12)
v St Mirren	(21/01/12)
v Hearts	(08/02/12)
v Inverness CT	(11/02/12)
v Motherwell	(25/02/12)
v Rangers	(25/03/12)
v St Johnstone	(01/04/12)
v Kilmarnock	(07/04/12)

6 substitute

v Hibernian	(24/07/11)
v Aberdeen	(07/08/11)
v Inverness CT	(24/09/11)
v Hibernian	(29/10/11)
v Dunfermline	(23/11/11)
v Dunfermline	(22/02/12)

4 goals

v St Mirren	(26/11/11)
v Kilmarnock	(24/12/11)
v Kilmarnock	(24/12/11)
v St Johnstone	(01/04/12)

2 Yellow Cards

v Aberdeen	(23/10/11)
v Hearts	(08/02/12)

1 Yellow Card

v St Mirren	(26/11/11)

stats correct as of April 7, 2012

"There's a strong squad at the minute and the players are doing well but you have to give the gaffer credit. All his decisions this year have worked well, even when he's left people out of the team or rotated it around, it always seems to work." - ANTHONY STOKES (January 2012)

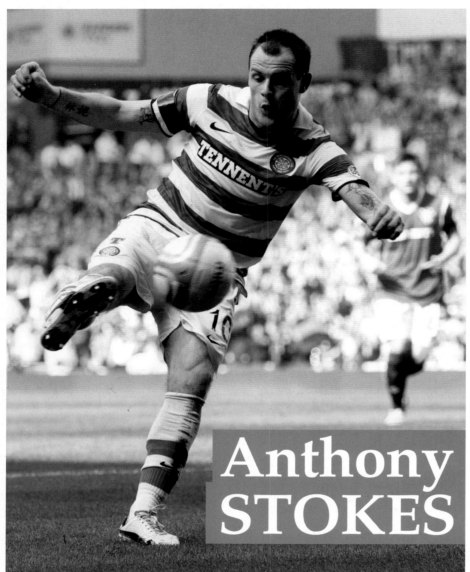

Anthony STOKES

2011/12 STATS

23 Appearances

v Hibernian	(24/07/11)
v Aberdeen	(07/08/11)
v Dundee United	(13/08/11)
v St Johnstone	(21/08/11)
v St Mirren	(28/08/11)
v Motherwell	(10/09/11)
v Inverness CT	(24/09/11)
v Kilmarnock	(15/10/11)
v Aberdeen	(23/10/11)
v Hibernian	(29/10/11)
v Motherwell	(06/11/11)
v Inverness CT	(19/11/11)
v Dunfermline	(23/11/11)
v St Mirren	(26/11/11)
v Dundee United	(04/12/11)
v Hearts	(10/12/11)
v Dunfermline	(02/01/12)
v Dundee United	(14/01/12)
v Hibernian	(19/02/12)
v Dunfermline	(22/02/12)
v Aberdeen	(03/03/12)
v Rangers	(25/03/12)
v St Johnstone	(01/04/12)

7 Substitute

v Rangers	(18/09/11)
v Hearts	(02/10/11)
v Rangers	(28/12/11)
v St Mirren	(21/01/12)
v Hearts	(08/02/12)
v Motherwell	(25/02/12)
v Kilmarnock	(07/04/12)

2 Yellow Cards

v Motherwell	(06/11/11)
v Rangers	(28/12/11)

11 Goals

v Hibernian	(24/07/11)
v Aberdeen	(07/08/11)
v Dundee United	(13/08/11)
v Kilmarnock	(15/10/11)
v Kilmarnock	(15/10/11)
v Motherwell	(06/11/11)
v Inverness CT	(19/11/11)
v Inverness CT	(19/11/11)
v Dunfermline	(02/01/12)
v Hibernian	(19/02/12)
v Aberdeen	(03/03/12)

stats correct as of April 7, 2012

THE Irishman has once again been a leading provider of goals this season, alongside fellow striker Gary Hooper. The two players have been vying for the title of top goalscorer for the second consecutive season, and it's a contest that could go down to the wire.

Both players have also supplied goals which are candidates for the goal of the season, though whether it's a drive from the edge of the box or a two-yard tap-in, like all strikers, Stokes and Hooper are just pleased to hit the back of the net.

It was Stokes who scored Celtic's first league goal of the league campaign, and it came at Easter Road against Hibernian back in July last season.

The Irishman has scored on every appearance at the ground since moving from Hibs to Celtic at the start of last season, and he began the new season as he meant to go on – with a superb finish. It took all of 13 minutes for Stokes to score. He controlled Kris Commons' free-kick at the far post, and from a tight angle, he lifted the ball over everyone and into the top corner of the net. It was a stunning strike and put Celtic on their way to the first victory of the 2011/12 season.

Since then, Stokes has continued to fire home the goals, with his two against Kilmarnock last October in the 3-3 draw at Rugby Park, vital in precipitating a comeback which helped to kick-start the Hoops' league challenge.

And Stokes will be hoping for another chance to net against Rangers before the season is out. He started the most recent clash at Ibrox, but was substituted after Cha Du-Ri's harsh red card.

Victor WANYAMA

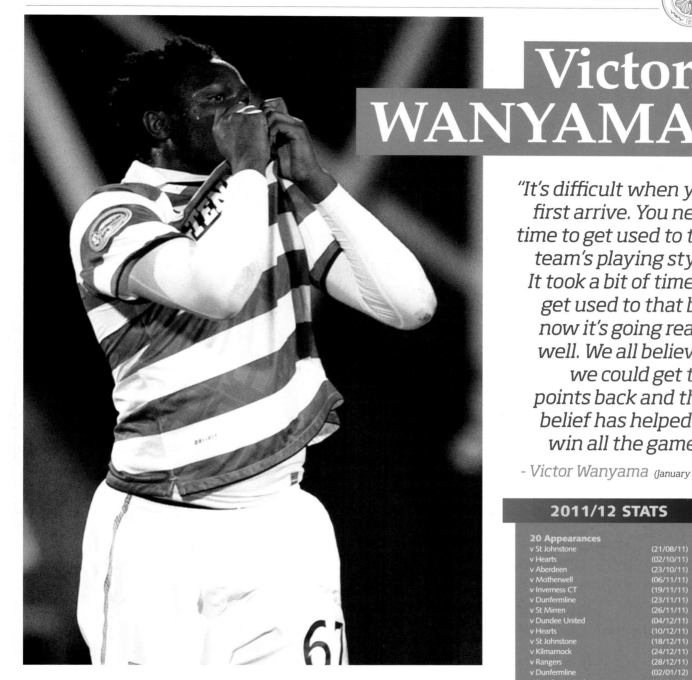

"It's difficult when you first arrive. You need time to get used to the team's playing style. It took a bit of time to get used to that but now it's going really well. We all believed we could get the points back and that belief has helped us win all the games."

- Victor Wanyama (January 2012)

2011/12 STATS

20 Appearances
v St Johnstone	(21/08/11)
v Hearts	(02/10/11)
v Aberdeen	(23/10/11)
v Motherwell	(06/11/11)
v Inverness CT	(19/11/11)
v Dunfermline	(23/11/11)
v St Mirren	(26/11/11)
v Dundee United	(04/12/11)
v Hearts	(10/12/11)
v St Johnstone	(18/12/11)
v Kilmarnock	(24/12/11)
v Rangers	(28/12/11)
v Dunfermline	(02/01/12)
v Dundee United	(14/01/12)
v St Mirren	(21/01/12)
v Hearts	(08/02/12)
v Inverness CT	(11/02/12)
v Hibernian	(19/02/12)
v Motherwell	(25/02/12)
v Rangers	(25/03/12)

4 Substitute
v Motherwell	(10/09/11)
v Kilmarnock	(15/10/11)
v Hibernian	(29/10/11)
v Aberdeen	(03/03/12)

4 Goals
v Hearts	(02/10/11)
v Dunfermline	(02/01/12)
v Dundee United	(14/01/12)
v Hearts	(08/02/12)

1 Yellow Card
v Kilmarnock	(15/10/11)

1 Red Card
v Rangers	(25/03/12)

stats correct as of April 7, 2012

CELTIC have discovered a player of superb football talent in Victor Wanyama, with the Kenyan internationalist, who is still only 20, quickly becoming one of the mainstays of the team since arriving from Belgian club, Beerschot, last summer. Since he really began to establish himself in the side, from around the start of October, Wanyama has rarely been out of the starting XI.

Whether at centre-half or in central midfield, his poise and power are attributes which have benefited the team, and he has played a crucial role in Celtic's success this season. When the Hoops were hit by a number of injuries in the central defence, it was Wanyama who stepped into the breach and performed superbly well.

And with Beram Kayal missing since the turn of the year through injury, it has been the young Kenyan who has provided the combative spirit within the central midfield area from where Celtic have built their success.

He's also chipped in with four goals. His first in the green and white Hoops was a spectacular effort against Hearts back in December which was enough to give Celtic a 1-0 victory, while he also scored in the 3-0 January win over Dunfermline, Celtic's first as league leaders. And he was also one of three midfielders, along with Scott Brown and Joe Ledley, who scored in the comprehensive 4-0 victory over Hearts at Tynecastle in February.

The only blip in an otherwise upward trajectory this season was the red card Wanyama received during the 3-2 derby defeat at Ibrox in March. But in his first season at the club, the 20-year-old has made a tremendous contribution and has the ability to continue to be a mainstay of the side for many years to come. in the Celtic squad as well.

Kelvin WILSON

"Everyone wants to play and everyone wants the same as you, so you hold no grudges. I'm going to continue to work hard and hopefully I will be called upon again soon. If and when that happens I will continue to do my best to try and fight for my place in the team."

KELVIN WILSON (February 2012)

2011/12 STATS

13 Appearances

v Hibernian	(24/07/11)
v Aberdeen	(07/08/11)
v Dundee United	(13/08/11)
v St Mirren	(28/08/11)
v Motherwell	(10/09/11)
v Rangers	(18/09/11)
v Hearts	(08/02/12)
v Inverness CT	(11/02/12)
v Hibernian	(19/02/12)
v Dunfermline	(22/02/12)
v Motherwell	(25/02/12)
v Aberdeen	(03/03/12)
v Kilmarnock	(07/04/12)

1 Substitute

v Kilmarnock	(24/12/11)

1 Yellow Cards

v Motherwell	(25/02/12)

stats correct as of April 7, 2012

KELVIN Wilson, like most of the central defenders at Celtic this season, has had to cope with a spell on the sidelines through injury.

Wilson suffered his Achilles injury during the League Cup win over Ross County, and it saw him out of the frame from the middle of September right through to February, though he had managed to push his way back into the squad by the turn of the year. The difficult part was then dislodging the incumbents in central defence.

As Celtic have closed in on the title, he has featured on a more regular basis, forming an impressive partnership with Thomas Rogne and showing some of the qualities that made Neil Lennon sign him.

Wilson's pace at the back is one of his main assets, and strikers have found him a tough opponent. Indeed, he was part of an impressive defensive unit which did not concede a single goal in the month of February, in five SPL games and one Scottish Cup tie. That helped the Hoops continue their remarkable run of victories as they extended their lead at the top of the table.

The manager has a number of different options in central defence, with Wilson battling it out with Rogne, Charlie Mulgrew, Daniel Majstorovic before he was injured, while Victor Wanyama has also shown his ability in that position. And the big Englishman will also be hoping to remain injury-free in the new campaign when the champions launch their bid to retain the title.

But like a number of players, Wilson will be delighted that his first season at the club has ended with a championship-winning medal in his possession, and a well-earned one at that.

No.20 Paddy McCOURT

VERY much a favourite with supporters, Paddy's mercurial talents are enough to get fans on their feet to cheer him. He's only appeared from the bench in the SPL this season, with his campaign also cluttered with some niggling injuries, but he is a player who is capable of turning a game with a moment of genius.

This is perhaps best illustrated with his introduction in the game against Motherwell on November 6, 2011. Celtic went into that game 15 points behind Rangers and knowing they could ill-afford to drop any more points.

And it was a trademark McCourt run,

jinking past several Motherwell players which put Anthony Stokes through and his ball in to Gary Hooper, who scored, was enough to give the Hoops a 2-1 win.

2011/12 STATS

10 Substitute	
v Dundee United	(13/08/11)
v St Johnstone	(21/08/11)
v Inverness CT	(24/09/11)
v Hearts	(02/10/11)
v Aberdeen	(23/10/11)
v Hibernian	(29/10/11)
v Motherwell	(06/11/11)
v Inverness CT	(19/11/11)
v Dunfermline	(23/11/11)
v St Mirren	(26/11/11)

stats correct as of April 7, 2012

No.46 Dylan McGEOUCH

THE young Celt announced his presence at the club in spectacular style in only his second appearance for the first-team. His debut had come in the 2-1 win over Motherwell at the beginning of November, and his second game was against St Mirren at the end of the month. And his goal in the 5-0 win was something special.

He won the ball on the edge of his own area and set off on a mazy run which ended just inside the St Mirren penalty area when the teenager fired home beyond the Saints' goalkeeper. McGeouch is definitely a young talent to watch for the future.

2011/12 STATS

4 Substitute	
v Motherwell	(06/11/11)
v St Mirren	(26/11/11)
v St Johnstone	(18/12/11)
v Aberdeen	(03/03/12)
1 Goal	
v St Mirren	(26/11/11)

stats correct as of April 7, 2012

No.12 Mark WILSON

MARK Wilson was one of Celtic's most consistent performers last season but

2011/12 STATS

4 Appearances	
v Hibernian	(24/07/11)
v Dundee United	(13/08/11)
v Rangers	(18/09/11)
v Hibernian	(29/10/11)
2 Substitute	
v St Johnstone	(21/08/11)
v Hearts	(02/10/11)
1 Yellow Cards	
v Rangers	(18/09/11)

stats correct as of April 7, 2012

his participation in the 2011/12 season has been hindered considerably by injury. At the start of November it was revealed that the player had to undergo knee surgery which ruled him out for at least three months.

Wilson is the longest-serving player at Celtic and his contribution over the years to the Celtic cause has been tremendous. A reliable performer when ever called upon, he will have been frustrated at his lack of involvement this campaign, but will have celebrated the title triumph as a player and as a supporter.

No.3 Emilio IZAGUIRRE

SCOTLAND'S Player of the Year for 2010/11 was a key member of Neil Lennon's squad and was expected to play a vital role again this season. But he suffered a terrible injury when he broke his ankle during the second game of the season – against Aberdeen at Pittodrie.

It meant that the Honduran internationalist missed the first half of the season, though his return to action on January 2, coming on as a substitute at East End Park against Dunfermline, was met with rapturous acclaim by the Celtic fans.

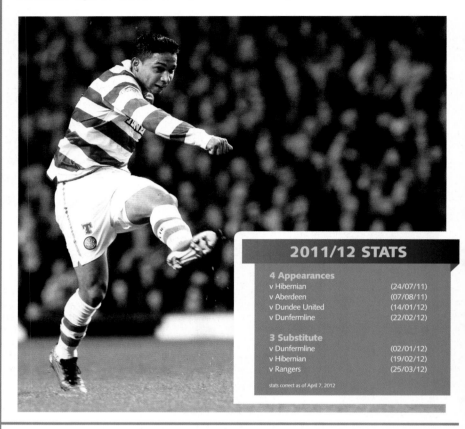

2011/12 STATS

4 Appearances

v Hibernian	(24/07/11)
v Aberdeen	(07/08/11)
v Dundee United	(14/01/12)
v Dunfermline	(22/02/12)

3 Substitute

v Dunfermline	(02/01/12)
v Hibernian	(19/02/12)
v Rangers	(25/03/12)

stats correct as of April 7, 2012

No.24 Lukasz ZALUSKA

THE Polish goalkeeper started Celtic's first three league games of the 2011/12 season, conceding just one goal, and that came in a 5-1 home win over Dundee United after he'd kept two clean sheets in the first two games of the campaign.

The arrival of Fraser Forster, which increased competition for places, saw the big Englishman take over the No.1 spot in the team. But Zaluska has remained an able deputy and his ability and professionalism were rewarded with a new three-year contract extension in March this year.

2011/12 STATS

3 Appearances

v Hibernian	(24/07/11)
v Aberdeen	(07/08/11)
v Dundee United	(13/08/11)

stats correct as of April 7, 2012

No.22 Glenn LOOVENS

THE Dutch defender is another one who has found his season disrupted by injury and after playing against Hearts in the middle of December, he didn't feature again until the beginning of April.

Loovens is in the last season of his contract with the club, and he now has a full set of domestic medals with Celtic, complementing the League Cup in 2009 and the Scottish Cup last season.

2011/12 STATS

9 Appearances

v Hibernian	(24/07/11)
v Rangers	(18/09/11)
v Inverness CT	(24/09/11)
v Aberdeen	(23/10/11)
v St Mirren	(26/11/11)
v Dundee United	(04/12/11)
v Hearts	(10/12/11)
v St Johnstone	(01/04/12)
v Kilmarnock	(07/04/12)

1 Goal

v Kilmarnock	(07/04/12)

1 Yellow Card

v St Mirren	(26/11/11)

stats correct as of April 7, 2012

No.14 Mo BANGURA

THE Sierra Leone striker joined Celtic from Swedish side AIK last summer, but injuries have had a big impact on his season, with him eventually requiring knee surgery in February which ruled him out of the rest of the campaign.

He had been troubled with a knee injury since November, and his participation up to the end of 2011 was mainly restricted to substitute appearances. Another player who will hoping for a good pre-season in order to start next season injury-free.

2011/12 STATS

1 Appearance
v Hearts	(02/10/11)

8 Substitute
v Motherwell	(10/09/11)
v Rangers	(18/09/11)
v Inverness CT	(24/09/11)
v Kilmarnock	(15/10/11)
v St Mirren	(26/11/11)
v Hearts	(10/12/11)
v St Johnstone	(18/12/11)
v Kilmarnock	(24/12/11)

stats correct as of April 7, 2012

THE Swedish internationalist arrived at Celtic Park during the January transfer window, having completed a full season with Norwegian side Rosenborg which finished in November. And it has taken the player a while to break through to the Celtic side, with him picking up a number of niggling injuries.

He made his debut in the 1-1 draw against Aberdeen at Pittodrie, when he was also booked, while he also started the match against St Johnstone. Lustig will also be hoping to head to Euro 2012 with Sweden.

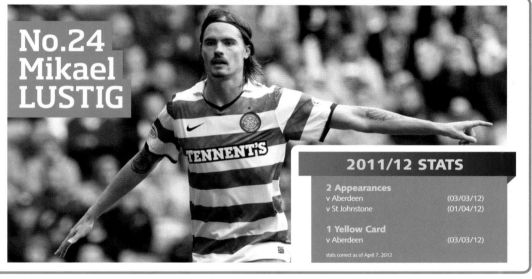

No.24 Mikael LUSTIG

2011/12 STATS

2 Appearances
v Aberdeen	(03/03/12)
v St Johnstone	(01/04/12)

1 Yellow Card
v Aberdeen	(03/03/12)

stats correct as of April 7, 2012

No.39 Andre BLACKMAN

THE young defender signed for Celtic in November last year after impressing in a number of bounce games. But he's another player who has found it difficult to break through into the first-team.

He made his debut in the 1-1 draw against Aberdeen, where he was unlucky to deflect the ball into his own net for Aberdeen's equaliser, while he made his first Celtic Park bow as a second-half substitute against St Johnstone.

2011/12 STATS

1 Appearance
v Aberdeen	(03/03/12)

2 Substitute
v St Johnstone	(01/04/12)
v Kilmarnock	(07/04/12)

stats correct as of April 7, 2012

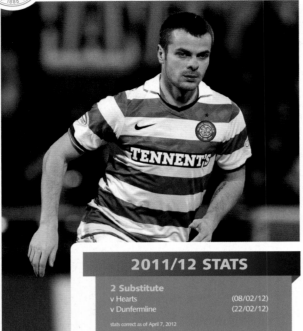

2011/12 STATS

2 Substitute
v Hearts (08/02/12)
v Dunfermline (22/02/12)

stats correct as of April 7, 2012

No.17 Pawel BROZEK

THE Polish internationalist joined Celtic on loan from Turkish side Trabzonspor at the end of January, but his participation so far has been restricted to two substitute appearances, the first of which came during the 4-0 victory over Hearts at Tynecastle.

Brozek will be hoping to make it into co-hosts Poland's Euro 2012 squad.

No.13 Shaun MALONEY

SHAUN Maloney made three appearances for Celtic this season before calling time on his second spell at the club, moving to Wigan Athletic on the final day of the summer transfer window.

His last appearance for the Hoops came in the home defeat against St Johnstone in August, while it wouldn't be until March this year before he made his first English Premier League appearance for Wigan.

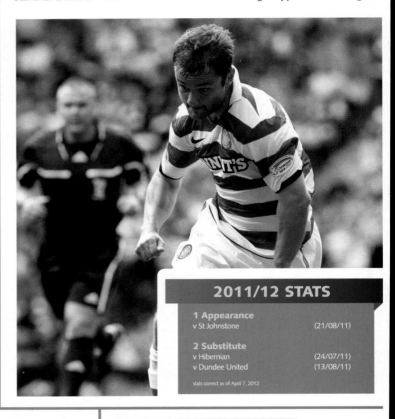

2011/12 STATS

1 Appearance
v St Johnstone (21/08/11)

2 Substitute
v Hibernian (24/07/11)
v Dundee United (13/08/11)

stats correct as of April 7, 2012

No.4 Badr EL KADDOURI

2011/12 STATS

5 Appearances
v Motherwell (10/09/11)
v Rangers (18/09/11)
v Inverness CT (24/09/11)
v Hearts (02/10/11)
v Inverness CT (19/11/11)

1 Substitute
v Kilmarnock (15/10/11)

1 Goal
v Rangers (18/09/11)

1 Yellow Card
v Inverness CT (19/11/11)

stats correct as of April 7, 2012

THE Moroccan internationalist joined Celtic on loan from Dynamo Kyiv in August last year, but he found it difficult to establish a place in the starting XI and he returned to the Ukrainian side in January.

During his time at Celtic, however, he did memorably score a derby goal against Rangers at Ibrox, his shot from outside the box fumbled by Allan McGregor.

No.56 Filip TWARDZIK

The 19-year-old Czech youngster enjoyed a dream first-team debut as he came on early in the second-half of the title-clinching game against Kilmarnock. He replaced Scott Brown in midfield, and produced an impressive performance as Celtic cruised to the title, eventually beating Killie 6-0.

The appearance is a real boost for the player, who is at Celtic along with his twin brother Patrik, and he will be hoping to push his way into Neil Lennon's squad on a more regular basis in the season ahead.

2011/12 STATS

1 Substitute
v Kilmarnock (07/04/12)

stats correct as of April 7, 2012